THE
FEMALE
INVESTOR

THE
FEMALE
INVESTOR

CREATING WEALTH
SECURITY
AND FREEDOM
THROUGH PROPERTY

**NICOLA McDOUGALL
AND KATE HILL**

WILEY

First published in 2022 by John Wiley & Sons Australia, Ltd

42 McDougall St, Milton Qld 4064
Office also in Melbourne

Typeset in Kepler Std 12pt/16pt

© John Wiley & Sons Australia, Ltd 2022

The moral rights of the authors have been asserted

ISBN: 978-0-730-39863-9

A catalogue record for this book is available from the National Library of Australia

Cover design by Wiley

Disclaimer

Nicola — For my mum, Adrienne, and my stepmum, Vickie, for teaching me courage and kindness; for my dad, Ian, who taught me many things, including about money; and for Josh and Nichole, who gave me love and hope.

Kate — for my partner in life, Jon, without whose unfailing love and support I would not be the person or investor I am today; for all the totally awesome clients over the years, both male and female, who continue to inspire me, who bring me joy, and who contribute to our giant investing family every day.

CONTENTS

CONTENTS

ABOUT THE AUTHORS

Nicola McDougall is a successful property investor, business owner, chairperson of the Property Investment Professionals of Australia, and an award-winning journalist. She is also the former editor of *Australian Property Investor* magazine and the co-founder of Bricks & Mortar Media. She has been involved in property research, analysis and reporting since 2006.

Kate Hill is an award-winning property mentor, qualified property investment adviser and buyer's agent. She has many years' first-hand experience researching real estate and making hundreds of successful property purchases for her clients. Many of Kate's fabulous female clients are living proof that women of all ages, backgrounds and circumstances can invest in property successfully.

INTRODUCTION

WHY YOU MUST ACT — NOW!

Hands up if you know a woman who is struggling financially to make ends meet. Maybe she is concerned about her financial future, or whether she's ever going to be able to afford to buy a property to call home. Perhaps she is nearing retirement and worrying about affording a home of her own.

She could be your sister, daughter, mother, aunty, mother-in-law, grandmother, cousin, or even a close female friend.

Perhaps she is single or in a relationship. She could also be divorced or even widowed. She may be in her 20s or her 60s — unfortunately, her age doesn't necessarily mean she will be financially secure.

We know plenty of women like this and we're sure you do, too.

Their situations — and their reasons why — vary widely because each of us is an individual who will experience challenges unique to us during the course of our life.

Sometimes they may not technically be struggling financially, but they worry about how they are going to retain their financial independence throughout their lives, or perhaps they're concerned about how they're going to fund their retirement — even if it's decades away.

Alas, their concerns are valid, because it's a fact that women generally remain less financially secure than men.

First up, there is the income pay gap between men and women, which stubbornly appears to not be changing significantly.

Then there is the stark difference in superannuation balances between men and women, which starts when workers are only in their 20s and never recovers.

And there are the increasing numbers of women who wind up homeless after a relationship breakdown or in retirement, because they were never able to create their own independent wealth or buy a home of their own.

Let's face it, half of all marriages still end in divorce and many women remain the primary caregivers of children — even more so during a pandemic, as it turned out.

And that means that if a women's 'forever' union ends in tatters, she's likely to be futilely playing financial catch-up for the rest of her working life.

Many women are worried about their lack of superannuation and about having to work until they are 80 instead of retiring. In fact, many women are forced to re-enter the workforce in their twilight years because they can't afford to live without doing so.

A recent retirement-income review repeatedly highlighted the inequitable outcomes for women, with women generally retiring with far fewer funds than men and also often living in poverty. What sort of end of life is that for anyone?

We want to be clear: this book is not anti-love, anti-marriage or anti-joint bank accounts.

The Female Investor is a book to help women stake their claim on the property market so they have the assets to improve their financial futures — regardless of whether they choose to partner up or not; whether they are single, married, divorced or widowed.

But it's not a book to teach women how to become property squillionaires. Rather, it's a guide that will teach you about the importance of maximising your income sooner, so you have more choices later on.

Even though the salary gap remains, the number of women investing in property is rising — but more still could be done to secure your personal financial future.

Fundamentally, this book is about women being clued up, taking charge and being proactive with their finances via strategic property investment — at any age.

The truth is that most women have experienced a world in which they were not encouraged to take care of themselves financially.

We want to help change that because it potentially leads to dependency upon a spouse, another family member, continued employment late in life or even the government for financial support.

So, *The Female Investor* is a rallying cry from women to women — from us to you — to motivate women of all ages to get educated, take charge of your own financial future, and become proactive enough to stake your claim on the property market — now!

THE FACTS

Here are some cold hard facts about the financial outcomes for women and men in our part of the world.

While most of these figures are drawn from Australian research, the situation is similar in most countries around the world — and the reality is that women are more likely than not to be financially inequitable with their male partners from the beginning of their relationships.

The lack of financial literacy for young children and teenagers is one reason for this imbalance, but one scary fact is that the financial outcomes for women and men in retirement start to solidify at the beginning of our working lives.

According to the Australian Government's *Women's economic security in retirement insight* paper (2020), even when women are in their late 20s, their superannuation balances are lower than men's.

The research found that women are on the back foot financially from the beginning of their careers and if they decide to have children, the gap just gets wider and wider, and it will keep growing throughout their lives.

By the time a woman retires in Australia, according to the insight paper, her average superannuation account balance is 17.4 per cent lower than a man's, which reflects the average superannuation account balances of $277 880 for women and $336 360 for men.

Even with Australia's superannuation scheme, which started in 1992, many women in Australia still retire without any funds whatsoever. Sadly, about one third of women wind up with no superannuation at all when they retire.

Superannuation was designed to help more people become financially independent in retirement, but most women and men still rely on the age pension as their primary source of income during that stage of their lives. According to the insight report, in 2017–18 about 70 per cent of women compared to 63 per cent of men relied on government pensions and allowances — these allowances could include payments such as an energy or essential-medical-equipment supplement, remote-area or carers allowance, or other benefit payments to help fund health and medical care.

Do you know how much the age pension is in Australia? In 2021, the maximum rate for a single person is less than $500 per week, including all potential allowances, which is hardly enough to live the life you've long dreamed about, is it?

For anyone under the age of about 50, retirement seems like a long way away, so we don't give it much thought, do we?

Of course everyone should enjoy their life rather than squirrel away every spare dollar for a stage of life that is decades in the future, but you can't ignore the truth forever.

This means that unless you prepare for retirement when you are youngish, including purchasing a strategically selected property (or perhaps two or three), then the outcome for you may be spending your twilight years in poverty. Here are some stark statistics from government research:

♦ Women are more likely than men to re-enter the workforce following retirement, often due to financial constraints.

♦ Women are twice as likely as men to sell their house and move to lower-cost accommodation because of tight financial circumstances in retirement.

The *Women's economic security in retirement insight* paper also reported more elderly women than men are living in poverty in Australia. Therefore, women are far more likely to face higher financial insecurity in retirement than men.

HOW CAN PROPERTY HELP?

One way that you can help to prevent this dire situation happening to you, as well as ensure you remain financially independent during your life, is to create wealth, security, and freedom through property.

We have written this book as a guide to help women understand how they can make their income work harder throughout their working lives, using property ownership as the vehicle.

While *The Female Investor* has been written with property investors — or landladies as we like to call them — predominantly in mind, you can apply this information to the purchase of any property, including your home.

WHY THE TERM 'LANDLADIES'?

The real-estate sector is riddled with over-the-top male references. So, we like to balance these out by taking back the term 'landladies' for female property investors.

We want every property you purchase to help you achieve superior capital growth over the medium to long term, as well as to assist with your future financial situation.

By understanding the key concepts, you will learn how to buy real estate with an investment mindset. This can help to maximise your returns as well as reduce the risks and kibosh your chances of buying a property lemon!

We believe that if, whatever your age, you understand property investment strategies thoroughly, you will be able to make more informed decisions to improve your financial outcomes in life. On top of that, you will be less likely to be stung by a property spruiker because you are educated (probably more than the spruiker!) about what makes an excellent property investment — and what does not.

WHY DOES IT MATTER?

Did you know that, according to the Grattan Institute's report *Money in Retirement — more than enough*, Australians who rent in the private market are more likely to suffer financial stress than homeowners, or renters in public housing? And this problem will get worse: on current trends, home ownership for over-65s will decline from 76 per cent today to 57 per cent by 2056.

Remember those paltry pension rates we mentioned before? Well, $500 per week probably doesn't seem so bad when most of us believe that we will have our home paid off by retirement. That is, if we even own a home.

Clearly, the scenario becomes much more difficult when a single woman is trying to pay rent out of her pension, even if the government throws her some 'rent assistance' to ease the financial burden.

There is no question that women have been forging their own paths for more than half a century now, with career progression, motherhood and independent wealth creation all worthy goals for each of us.

But, somewhere along the way, home ownership rates have started to slip, with high property prices likely to be one of the reasons why. However, as you will learn in *The Female Investor*, even women on modest incomes can (and should) purchase property — and preferably when they are single and in their 20s ... but much more on that later.

According to the *Women's economic security in retirement insight paper* (2020), the largest asset held by Australians in retirement has traditionally been property. However, the number of Australians, including retirees, who own their home has been decreasing.

Across the age groups 15 years and over, the proportion of individuals who owned their home and were not paying a mortgage was 30 per cent in 2015–16, which was down from 35 per cent in 2003–04. Similarly, the insight paper found that 76 per cent of individuals aged 65 years and over were homeowners and not paying off a mortgage in 2015–16, which was down from 79 per cent in 2003–04.

These percentages probably don't look too bad at a glance, but when you turn them around the other way, this means that nearly a quarter of all Australians are either renting or paying off a mortgage after they turn 65 years of age — up from 21 per cent about 12 years before. Could you imagine having to do that with little to no superannuation, plus living week to week, barely surviving on the pension?

It's difficult to determine why so many people are still paying off a mortgage in retirement, but it's likely due to a lack of financial literacy to start off with. One way that you can prevent this situation becoming your story is by joining the property-ownership ranks earlier, including adding one or two properties to your portfolio over the years — these can be sold to pay down mortgage debt or to create cash flow in retirement.

Together, we have decades of experience in the property investment sector, including both being successful property investors ourselves. Over the years, we've learned what works and what doesn't.

We've stuffed up and bought the wrong type of dwellings, or purchased in inferior locations and paid dearly for our boo-boos. Nicola sometimes even calls her property investment strategy 'scrappy' for the wheeling and dealing she has had to do to get the deal done. You can hopefully learn from our mistakes and never have to watch the value of your so-called asset plummet. We have walked the talk, and we've experienced the ups and downs that can come with owning property for decades — we're still standing and we're still smiling!

We believe that if this book can motivate, encourage or nudge even one woman to invest in her first, second, or even her third, property then that is success to us.

Our wish is to create a whole community of women who are taking action to secure their own financial futures — and who will inspire the next generation along the way.

WHAT WILL YOU LEARN?

We're going to be honest with you throughout this book, which means that we won't be providing a step-by-step approach that you can simply follow then retire to the Bahamas!

Rather, you must consider everything you read in these pages as the start of your education on property investment strategy. You will learn what we believe you should do to improve your chances of maximising your returns and minimising the risks. But we don't believe there is a cookie-cutter or one-size-fits-all model that suits absolutely everyone.

In fact, creating wealth, security and freedom through property is all about creating a bespoke model that is the best fit for you as an individual. There is very little out there to educate women about the basics of property investment, written by women like us, who have been there and done that ourselves.

Over the next 11 chapters, we will guide you through the beginnings of your strategic-property-investment education. We have tried to provide as much detail as possible on the key elements required for you to become a successful investor of property. That said, there is not enough room to cover off on every single detail or possibility in great depth. However, you can learn heaps more via thefemaleinvestor.com.au and via our podcast, too!

We want all women, whether you are buying a home or an investment, to understand the fundamentals of property as an investment vehicle, so your funds and your real estate asset can work the very hardest for you over the years — whether you are living in it or renting it out.

So, let's get started, shall we?

CHAPTER 1

WHO CAN HELP

Getting your team on board

Long before you even start looking at property porn (as we like to call it) online, you should make sure you have the right team of people in your corner.

Remember that you're probably about to spend hundreds of thousands of dollars on an income-producing asset that will help set you up for life! Why wouldn't you seek out the opinion of some professionals who do this sort of stuff every day of every week?

YOUR EXPERT TEAM

Skimping on paying for expert advice is one of the biggest mistakes investors can make — female or male — no matter how experienced they think they are.

Yes, you'll pay for their services in the short term, but their advice can save you megabucks over the long term, and can also save you from making even more costly mistakes in the future. If someone is offering you their 'advice' supposedly for free, you should run a country mile, because they are only interested in their wealth creation and not yours!

Here is an overview of who we think you may need on your expert team, depending on your individual requirements.

MORTGAGE BROKER

A mortgage broker is someone who liaises with you and the banks, or other lenders, to arrange a home loan for you.

Mortgage brokers are trained and qualified to provide you with mortgage-broking advice. By law, they must act in your best interests when suggesting a loan and a loan structure for you. Generally, it doesn't cost you, the borrower, any money to consult with a mortgage broker and we believe the service they provide — and the headaches they can prevent — is often underrated.

All banks and lenders pay the broker a commission for 'selling' their products. Some brokers get paid a standard fee regardless of what loan they recommend. Other brokers get a higher fee for offering certain loans.

Sometimes a broker will charge you a fee directly — instead of, or as well as, the lender's commission. If you're not sure whether you're getting a good deal, ask around or look online to see what other brokers charge, if anything.

A good mortgage broker works with you to understand your needs and goals. They will:

- work out what you can afford to borrow

- find options to suit your situation

- talk to you about many different banks, lenders, and available loan products.

Conversely, if you go directly to the bank, that bank will only ever talk to you about their own loan products. Mortgage brokers are independent advisers, whereas the banks are not.

Getting a good recommendation is super important. Always check their qualifications and whether they belong to their industry body or association.

ACCOUNTANT

A great accountant will do a lot more than simply prepare your tax returns at the end of the financial year. Most people don't ask them enough questions before they do anything.

When you're buying investment properties, you'll need advice on:

◆ what ownership structures to buy your investment property in

◆ what marginal tax rate to apply to your cash-flow calcs

◆ what you can and cannot claim a tax deduction on.

You should talk to your accountant about tax planning, too— it's not just about the next six months, it's about the next five years and beyond. Are you about to get married? Are you about to go on maternity leave? Are you about to change jobs? The answers to all these questions will make a difference to your property ownership and the costs of holding the property.

Get their advice and input before you start buying. Don't present them with a property that you've bought, hoping for a retrospective solution, because a seemingly simple mistake can be costly to fix.

Ideally, your accountant should also be a property investment specialist. Again, check their qualifications and whether they belong to their industry body or association, including the Property Investment Professionals of Australia (PIPA).

FINANCIAL PLANNER/ADVISER

A financial planner or adviser will help you plan your financial goals.

They will:

◆ conduct a financial health check on you

◆ ask you about a million questions

◆ come up with a plan to make your goals a reality

◆ help you to understand what you need to put in place and what's involved in meeting your future goals

They can:

◆ help with your household budgeting

◆ set up a savings strategy

◆ compile a comprehensive investment plan to ensure you're heading in the right direction

◆ advise you on what types of insurance will protect you and your family.

They also have the capacity and licences to make investments for you, such as managed funds and superannuation advice.

At some stage, it's always advisable to engage with an independent, fee-for-service financial planner who can look at your situation holistically and advise you about estate and retirement planning.

Again, make sure you check their qualifications and whether they belong to their industry body or association. We can't stress enough how important this is!

BUYER'S AGENT

A buyer's agent is a licensed professional who works for you, the buyer, and acts on your behalf to search, evaluate and negotiate a property purchase. They don't sell real estate. They are engaged independently and paid by the buyer to independently act on their behalf.

The key difference between a selling agent and a buyer's agent is who they represent — by law, in Australia an agent cannot act for and accept a commission from both parties in the same property transaction. Some of the things that a buyer's agent can help with:

◆ search for a property for you

◆ evaluate and complete all the due diligence on the listings available for sale

◆ negotiate the property purchase price and terms

◆ oversee the contract of sale

◆ assist throughout the settlement process

◆ oversee and arrange due diligence such as building and pest inspections, and survey and engineering reports.

By using an experienced buyer's agent, you can:

◆ gain an edge by having your own advocate who is representing your interests 100 per cent

- save time spent searching for and analysing property

- negotiate to obtain the best price and terms

- source the correct property in the right location with better prospects for capital growth and/or rental yield

- eliminate stress by having one representative looking after your needs, rather than dealing with several different selling agents.

If you're buying an investment property, then ideally you need a buyer's agent who is also a qualified property investment adviser and who has a thorough understanding of your investment goals, who can calculate cash flows for you, and assess your risks and needs. This is a critical part of the process. Again, check their bona fides before working with them.

QUALIFIED PROPERTY INVESTMENT ADVISER

A qualified property investment adviser (QPIA) performs a different role from that of a buyer's agent. Ideally, you want both of these skill sets rolled into one person.

Property is not an asset class recognised by the Australian Securities and Investments Commission, so, remarkably, the property investment industry remains unregulated in Australia. This means that anyone who feels like it can dish out property investment 'advice' with pretty much zero qualifications or repercussions if that advice is, ahem, 'dodgy'.

This sorry state of affairs has meant that the property investment space in Australia is riddled with spruikers who sell inferior property in underwhelming locations, with their only motivation being to line their own pockets, rather than work in the best interests of the people they're selling to.

All is not lost, though — you can seek out professionals who have gone to the trouble of getting themselves qualified, because they care about the financial outcomes and the financial futures of their clients, not just selling you a property on their books.

Go to the PIPA website and you'll find a growing list of QPIAs who have done just that. An ethical QPIA should take the time to:

◆ understand your situation

◆ conduct risk profiling on you

◆ recommend a strategy that suits you.

A growing number of mortgage brokers, accountants and even conveyancers are QPIAs, too.

SALES AGENT

These people get a bit of a bad rap, like used-car salespeople and journalists, and most of them really are decent and lovely people with a job to do. Are there some bad apples? Of course there are. Are some better than others? Sure, but you can say that about every industry.

When someone wants to sell a property that they own they will likely engage a selling agent to do that for them. A selling agent has a legal obligation to act in the best interests of the seller. This is called their fiduciary duty. The agent would generally:

◆ advise the seller on what price the property might sell for based on recent comparable sales

◆ advise on and then handle the sales and marketing strategy

◆ negotiate with potential buyers

◆ often (but not always) handle some of the post-purchase process, such as issuing contracts of sale and liaising with the buyer's mortgage broker and conveyancer to ensure smooth settlement.

When buying property, we can't always choose the agent we work with. The agent is chosen by the seller, not the buyer. You're simply choosing the property you're interested in and will then have to deal with the agent assigned to that sale. However, that doesn't mean they're not useful to you. A good agent will know their area inside out, will know many owners and sellers of property, and may have access to listings that haven't come onto the open market yet.

If you have a good relationship with local agents, then they can tell you when new listings come their way — sometimes before they're publicly advertised. So it pays to be courteous and treat them with respect, because you never know when you may need to negotiate with them. You never know when you may need them to present you and your offer to their client, and if they don't like you, they may not do that in a way most beneficial to you. So be nice!

CONVEYANCER OR SOLICITOR

A professional and licensed conveyancer or solicitor will handle all the legalities of purchasing or selling a property for you.

Signing that contract of sale to purchase a property is really only the beginning of the process, and there's also good reason to engage with them before you sign on the dotted line. The conveyancer or solicitor will handle a range of legal matters to ensure your rights are protected and you meet all your legal obligations, so that the sale goes smoothly.

Keep in mind that the conveyancing process is different in each state in Australia, so you'll need someone who's licensed to operate in the state that you're buying in. You will need to enlist their service to help check over the contract of sale and other related contract-associated documents before you sign them. They can also help to advise you on the right clauses and special conditions you might want to add or take out, so, that you get the best possible contract terms to suit you.

A conveyancer's job is to:

♦ carry out all the relevant searches required

♦ prepare the settlement documents

♦ conduct title searches (to ensure the property belongs to the seller and confirm whether any debts or liabilities exist on the property)

♦ run local authority searches (to check whether there are any future plans to develop the area upon which the land lies, e.g. build a motorway or develop an apartment complex)

♦ perform strata searches (if you're buying an apartment then you'll want to find out whether the building is running on a deficit or is able to sustain the running of the complex)

♦ find out many more vital pieces of information and manage all the transfer documents

♦ liaise with your bank or broker to ensure the property is rightfully and legally transferred to your name, or from your name if selling, on time.

A solicitor can also give you legal advice around ownership structures, which a conveyancer cannot. Check their quals before proceeding.

PROPERTY MANAGER

Property managers are the middle person between the owner of the property and the renter.

A property manager will generally:

+ advertise the property for rent

+ screen tenants

+ process tenant applications

+ manage rent paid

+ maintain and repair property

+ stay current with landlord-tenant laws

+ keep property records

+ keep accounts.

However, before you've even bought the property, they can assist you in these ways:

+ evaluate potential listings

+ inspect properties on your behalf

+ advise on potential maintenance items

+ provide you with a rent appraisal on each property you're considering making an offer on.

Property managers are an invaluable part of the process, and it pays to have them on board before you start your property search. There's way more on these fabulous people throughout this book!

QUANTITY SURVEYOR

Quantity surveyors document and assess each asset within a property and calculate the depreciable value to ensure that the investor maximises their tax deductions. This would include, for example:

♦ measuring rooms using a laser measurer

♦ recording an asset's brand or model number

♦ photographing improvements at the property.

The information they record from their inspection is used to prepare what's called a tax depreciation schedule, which outlines the depreciation deductions that can be claimed every year at tax time. It's a must-have for every property investor who owns property of a certain age and can make a difference to your cash flow — especially in the first few years of property investment ownership.

BUILDING AND PEST INSPECTOR

A building and pest inspection is a vital part of the property purchase process that you can, and should, have completed before or during the process of buying; again, depending on which state you're buying in. The report will list any signs of termite or pest infestation or damage, and will highlight any significant building defects or problems such as rising damp, movement in the walls (cracking), safety hazards, or a faulty roof.

The inspectors will check and inspect things like:

- the interior and exterior of the building

- the roof space

- the under-floor space, if there is one

- the roof exterior

- the land on which the property has been constructed

- garages, sheds, drainage, retaining walls, fencing etc.

You can also ask for a particular item or part of the property to be inspected, such as visible signs of asbestos or operable smoke alarms.

Building and pest inspectors are an integral part of your buying process, so that you know what you're getting into. It's all about buying with your eyes wide open, and not getting any nasty shocks six months down the track. One last time — check their credentials before engaging them.

CASE STUDY: CLAIRE'S STORY

A lovely lady called Claire came to see Kate a couple of years ago. She's a more mature lady and she wanted to purchase an investment property to add to her portfolio.

What Kate thought was so amazing about Claire was that she already owned six (yes, you read that correctly) other investment properties. She still had debt on some of these properties, she owned some of them outright, and as they were also scattered across six different states in Australia, she had never actually visited any of them. They had been carefully selected, purchased, and held in her portfolio for the long term.

Claire's husband of 30 years had passed away fairly recently, so she'd gone through quite the process in terms of rearranging her finances and all the legalities. But here she was knocking on Kate's door raring to go with the next one. She knew what she wanted to achieve with her next property and had some specific criteria to follow in terms of purchase price and rent return.

There really is no limit to what women like Claire, who have a clear plan and know their own risk profiles, can achieve. It was a complete joy to bring Claire's dreams of real financial freedom one step closer to reality.

TO-DO LIST

- [ ] Start thinking about the experts who can help you.

- [ ] Ask for recommendations from successful investors.

- [ ] Make sure you check out their credentials before contacting them.

- [ ] Ask for testimonials — if they hesitate, well, it's time to keep looking.

CHAPTER 2
HOW TO SAVE

Finance is not a dirty word

Your family may not have talked much about money, right?

Most of us certainly didn't learn much about it in school, which is thankfully changing, so that the next generation will be more clued up about money management than most of us ever were.

Talking about finance became a dirty word at some point in history, it seems. It likely had something to do with the long-held power imbalances in relationships, such as the fact that most women stayed home and looked after the children once they were born. Many never went back to work again because of lack of opportunity or, ahem, permission.

The 1960s and 1970s started to change all that, with women heading back into the workforce in record numbers.

When we think about the hundreds of years of mainly men making all the money, then, women really haven't had long in the grand old scheme of things to learn how to make the most of theirs, have they?

One of our motivations is to help change that, so that women of any age can understand how to take charge of their own financial futures — whether they decide to partner up with a man or a woman, or not at all.

We think that improving financial literacy can only be positive for society and if we can help more women become financially independent by way of strategic property investment, then our time on this earth will have been used wisely.

We're not going to instruct you on what is the best way to invest in property, because it will be different for each and every woman.

Each of us has different hopes, dreams, and aspirations, financial or otherwise, don't we? We are all individuals who have diverse careers, incomes and responsibilities. Some of us have children and others do not. A number of us will get married in our 20s, others in our 40s, and some of us not at all.

You can see where we are going with this, can't you? Your property investment journey should be tailored and unique to you personally as well as your phase of life, and your wealth creation and retirement goals. Anyone who tells you otherwise should be given a wide berth.

Our hope is that you understand all of the ins and outs of property investment so you can make your own informed decision on what is the best path for you. Never again will a woman be hoodwinked by a spruiker if we have our way!

The first step for many women is deciding to prioritise their own financial future. The second is to save that first deposit which — we're not going to lie — has always been bloody hard.

SAVING A DEPOSIT

Most of us don't have a Great-Aunt Mildred who conveniently dies and leaves us a wad of cash to buy our first property with, do we?

In fact, we hope that more women will learn how to rely on their own endeavours to improve their financial lot in life, rather than banking on an obscure elderly relative, a long-lost cousin, or their future, or current, partner.

But let's get down to business.

Property prices generally only go one way over the decades — and that is up. It can seem impossible to ever save fast enough to keep pace with rising prices, which is one reason why so many women give up at the first hurdle.

But there are ways and means to help you save that first deposit, including the fact that it doesn't have to be the mythical 20 per cent of the purchase price that many people think it does — although that is always advisable. You do need to show genuine savings to lenders.

Saving funds for a deposit is a great exercise in budgeting and money management that will hold you in good stead for the rest of your days.

5 SIMPLE STEPS TO SAVE A DEPOSIT

Here are some simple steps you can take to help you reach and clear that first savings hurdle.

1. CUT BACK – BUT DON'T FORGET TO LIVE

Most of us have higher discretionary spending than we realise — especially with the ease of online ordering of everything from clothes to food to wine. Saving a deposit takes discipline, delayed gratification and plenty of patience, which means you may need to cut back on some of the things you like to enjoy the most for a while.

Perhaps, instead of meeting up with friends for drinks and dinner at a restaurant, you take turns to host at each other homes instead? Maybe save ordering from a food delivery service for a Friday-night treat, so that you can celebrate the end of the week as well as the extra money in your bank account?

Working with a finance professional may be an idea to calculate how much of your income can be diverted to savings. You might be surprised with the result.

2. FROM LITTLE THINGS, BIG THINGS GROW

Set aside a certain amount from your salary or wages every time you are paid — and we mean on the day that it hits your bank account! Ideally, you should automate this so that you don't even notice it leaving your account and you don't have the chance to spend it.

You may need some expert advice, including on creating a budget, to help you determine what is a realistic amount that you can save. The last thing you want to do is try to save too much and leave yourself short when bills arrive, or it all gets too hard and you simply give up.

3. OUT OF SIGHT, OUT OF MIND

Online banking means it's easier than ever before to park those savings in a separate bank account. Now, they won't really be out of sight and out of mind, but they won't be in your everyday transaction account either, beckoning you enticingly.

Ideally, they could be in an account where those savings can work harder for you, too — perhaps in an offset account, if you already have a mortgage, to lower your interest rate repayments, or simply in an interest-earning one that can add some extra dollars to the balance without you doing anything else.

4. MONEY-MAKERS

Another way to help supercharge your savings is to simply earn more money, perhaps from a part-time gig for a period of time.

Maybe instead of ordering from a food delivery service, you work for them from time to time instead? There's a huge number of options out there these days.

Another strategy to help you save more money could be creating personal challenges, such as not eating out for two weeks, or signing up for Dry July or similar, which will likely end up being good for your liver as well as your purse!

5. GETTING TO GRIPS WITH GRANTS

There are usually a variety of different first home owner grants on the table, which can help to shave thousands off purchasing costs (such as by reduced stamp duty fees in Australia), as well as funds that you can potentially use towards a deposit. Of course, there is no such thing as free money, so these sorts of grants often come with a number of criteria that must be met.

In Australia, these types of grants are usually administered by your state government, so it's best to do your research on its official website when reading up on what is currently available — they do tend to change quite regularly.

THE LOWDOWN ON LOANS

Mortgage or property loan pre-approvals have become more and more popular over the years — and for very good reason. Back in the 'old days' many buyers usually didn't even bother talking to a mortgage broker or their bank until they had put an offer on a property and were frantically trying to get their finances in order to finalise the deal. Sounds stressful, right? It was!

In hot market conditions and when buying at auction, a loan pre-approval is non-negotiable to ensure that you are 'purchase ready' and can make an offer or a bid with confidence, knowing that you have the funds to back up your bravado.

However, we also recommend loan pre-approvals for first-time buyers and anyone re-entering the property market. This will not only help reduce stress when buying, but also set the budget for your potential property purchase. Plus, it can make the difference between being the successful buyer or not when there is far more demand than supply in a market.

> **HOT TIP**
>
> Don't go too crazy on the pre-approval front. Applying for multiple pre-approvals and multiple times can negatively impact your credit score. Keep in mind also that sometimes the banks won't issue pre-approvals like they used to because they may be short-staffed — like during the COVID-19 pandemic — or their policies are changing every other day. This can be challenging, so always talk to your trusted mortgage broker about the best strategy for you before marching into the nearest bank.

The number of people using mortgage brokers has skyrocketed over the past couple of decades — for very good reason, if you ask us.

- ◆ Most professional mortgage brokers have access to a large number of lenders who may fit your individual financial requirements.

- ◆ They can also be on your team throughout your property investment journey.

Now we're not saying there is anything wrong with big banks, because your mortgage broker may find that one of the major lenders is right for you.

What we're saying is that going direct to a bank will probably not provide you with all of the options available to you. A mortgage broker, on the other hand, will have knowledge about, and access to, lenders who are the perfect fit for someone who might be self-employed, a single parent, or who has a smallish deposit.

When it comes to successful property investment, experience counts. Work with a finance expert who has runs on the board, and who preferably also knows about property investment — we're thinking, for example, a QPIA.

There is a saying in the industry that property investment is as much a game about finance as it is about real estate, because without the funds to buy, well, you can't do anything at all, can you?

I CAN BORROW HOW MUCH?

Anyone who has been investing for as long as we both have can tell a story about the time a bank was going to lend them $1.7 million when they only asked for $700 000, or the time that they wouldn't give them anything at all, even though their numbers were fine (thanks, COVID-19 pandemic). The reality of the situation is that the lending environment can, and does, turn on a dime because of a bunch of factors too lengthy to list here.

One month you may qualify for a loan and the next you may not, because of levers being pulled at the top of the food chain to speed up, or slow down, lending. This can depend on what's happening in the economy, or whether local property markets are deemed too hot to handle (like Sydney back in 2017).

Loan pre-approvals generally only have a limited shelf life because of this relative fluidity of the lending environment, as well as your own personal financial circumstances.

Borrowing capacity is the amount of funds that a lender is prepared to offer you to finance a property, depending on your income, expenses, deposit size and a bunch of other variables best left to the finance experts to explain to you in more detail.

So we recommend meeting with a mortgage broker at the start of your journey — you can then understand how much your likely borrowing capacity will be if you were to purchase sooner rather than later.

A mortgage broker can also help you determine the size of deposit you will likely need to qualify for finance in a particular property price bracket.

HOT TIP You can decide to borrow less than the bank will lend you. Just because they're throwing $1 million at you, doesn't mean you should spend it!

Having these conversations early can help set you on the right path to save funds for a deposit. It will also ensure your finances are squeaky clean when it comes time to apply for finance by doing things such as reducing the number of credit and store cards, and paying down or paying off personal loans — these can all negatively impact your borrowing capacity.

If you are re-entering the market after a period — perhaps following a relationship breakdown or the death of a partner — and already own a property, then a broker will also be able to help you understand how much equity you may have available to recycle into another property. We're going to talk about this element in chapter 6.

WHAT IS EQUITY?

Equity is the difference between the current value of a property and its outstanding mortgage, minus about 20 per cent of the value, which the lender likes to retain as a safety net.

For example, a property valued at $800 000 with a mortgage of $400 000 may have about $260 000 in equity that could be used to purchase another real estate asset.

$$\$800\,000 - 20\% = \$640\,000$$

$$-\$400\,000 = \$240\,000$$

WHAT'S WITH ALL THE ACRONYMS?

It's about this time in a new, or returned, property buyer's journey that they start to come across a whole bunch of terms and acronyms that it will pay for them to understand. And, when it comes to finance, the two big ones to do with your mortgage are LVR and LMI.

LVR is short for loan-to-valuation ratio — the ratio of your property loan compared to the value of the property you want to buy. So, if you purchase a property for $500 000 and you have a deposit of $100 000 — 20 per cent of the purchase price — then you have an LVR of 80/20.

Most first-time buyers don't have a 20 per cent deposit, because it is difficult to save such a high figure while also paying rent and normal household expenses. However, just because you have less than this figure as a deposit doesn't mean you won't qualify for a property loan, although it might mean you need to change where and what you are looking at buying (more about that in later chapters). Your broker will be able to provide advice on the lenders best suited to borrowers with higher LVRs of, say, 90/10 — 90 per cent (loan) versus 10 per cent (deposit).

In Australia, the catch is that you will need to pay something called lenders mortgage insurance (LMI) — yep, another new acronym to learn. LMI is a fee that is charged to borrowers with a deposit smaller than 20 per cent of the purchase price of the property.

Now, it might sound like it's an insurance policy for you, but it's not. It's insurance for the lender via an additional fee from the buyer because of the perceived higher risk in lending money to a borrower with a smaller deposit.

Here's the truth about LMI: no one likes paying it, but if it makes the difference between you getting into the market sooner — or even at all — then it can be used to your advantage. That's because paying LMI, which can also be capitalised (added) onto the loan, is often a small price to pay compared to the potential capital growth the property could earn you over the additional years you will own it. For property investors, having larger property loans can also provide tax advantages, given it is only the interest component of a mortgage that is tax deductible — you should discuss this with your accountant.

NICOLA TELLS:

HOW LMI HELPED PAY FOR A PENTHOUSE

I bought the first three properties for my portfolio when I was single, earning an average wage.

My first one, in 2007, was when the Brisbane property market was going through a rare growth phase. There were buyers everywhere and not much stock on the ground. The deposit I had saved wasn't enough to secure me anything likely to improve my finance lot in life.

So my younger brother and I decided to buy something together, with some help from our parents, and I made peace with paying LMI to make it happen.

I bought my brother out of his share of that property a few years later. I ended up borrowing against that property twice more to add to my portfolio.

I recently sold that first one, which was a townhouse in a rather bland (at the time) middle-ring suburb, and it has helped finance my dream property — a riverfront penthouse.

UNDERSTANDING MORTGAGE REPAYMENTS

A key decision to make when you're applying for a mortgage, or refinancing an existing one, is whether you want to have fixed or variable interest rates on the loan. There is no right or wrong answer to this question, because it will depend on what the best strategy is for you at the time.

A fixed interest rate is usually a lower percentage than variable. Sometimes this can provide financial peace of mind, especially if there may be a change to your income in the short term, such as changing jobs, studying, or having your first, or your next, child.

However, fixed-rate mortgages generally have a number of limitations, including restricting how much of the principal loan amount you can pay off over the fixed-rate period, which is generally between one and five years.

A property loan with a variable interest rate means that the interest rate can go up or down depending on the monetary policy of the Reserve Bank of Australia (or equivalent) as well as your lender's own interest rate movements. There's no question that choosing between a fixed rate and a variable one can mean thousands of dollars in savings over the life of the loan, which your mortgage broker can outline

Loan structure is just as important, though, if you ask us.

Many borrowers get so fixated on interest rates that they forget about loan structure entirely, so they rush in and sign up with a lender for a five-year fixed rate just because they're the cheapest, without reading the fine print. Then not long after, their circumstances change unexpectedly — life is like that — and they find themselves stuck with a loan that they can't change or refinance because the only thing they considered was the super-low interest rate that was dangled like a golden carrot in front of them at the time.

BREAK FEES – WHAT ARE THEY?

You need to be aware of break fees, so here goes.

A break fee represents the bank's loss if a borrower repays their loan early or switches their loan product, interest rate or repayment type during a fixed-rate period.

When the bank agrees to lend you money at a fixed interest rate, they obtain money from the 'money market' out there at wholesale interest rates based on you making your repayments as agreed until the end of the fixed-rate period. If you don't, and wholesale interest rates change, then the bank may make a loss. They try and recoup this loss by charging you a break fee.

These considerations are why it's vital to consider — as best you can — all your options, as well as the likelihood of things happening for the next few years. Talk to a finance expert who can advise you on what they believe may happen with interest rates in the next couple of years. No one has a crystal ball, but a professional with their finger on the financial pulse should have an idea of where interest rates are headed in the near future.

On the whole, interest rates generally don't move up or down rapidly unless there is something serious happening, like a global health pandemic or a global financial crisis!

During both of these events, interest rates were lowered rapidly to underpin, and stimulate, the economy during the resultant turbulent economic times, but that is far from normal.

It's important to keep in mind that these scenarios are extremely rare, so please don't lose sleep over what interest rates may, or may not, do in the future. Rather, do your best to secure the optimal loan for your individual circumstances as well as your current and future property investment plans.

Of course, mortgages do need to be repaid at some point, whether it's through your own mortgage repayments, rental income, or selling the property. Most property owners opt for a principal and interest mortgage over 25 or 30 years, which means they are making regular repayments that will eventually pay off the debt.

On the other hand, investors tend to use interest-only repayments, because only the interest is a tax deduction, but also to reduce the additional cash-flow demands from their own bank accounts (we talk more about this in chapter 8) after rental income.

KATE TELLS:

TO FIX OR NOT TO FIX?

Many years ago, I was advised to fix all of my loans at over 6 per cent (which seemed good at the time) for three years – right before interest rates started falling.

I was totally stuck and couldn't get out of it without massive break fees. I couldn't pay the loans down, even if I wanted to, because of the fixed-loan restrictions. It killed me for over three years as I watched interest rates drop and drop and drop – and there was me paying bloody 6 per cent! If only I'd left a portion of it variable, I would've felt a bit happier and left myself with some flexibility to pay the loans down.

My finance blunder taught me to listen to advisers who know what they're talking about, who aren't in it for themselves, and who can help you plan out your future borrowings and life goals.

CASE STUDY: LISA'S STORY

Kate has known Lisa for some time. Lisa started investing on her own some years back and made some mistakes along the way, but always kept going because she never lost sight of the ultimate goal — financial independence.

Lisa's first goal was to pay off her home, a unit she'd bought when she was younger and was now living in with her partner. She did this and called Kate the day that she made her final payment with such excitement that it was infectious.

This gave her the freedom to not only leverage off the equity she had in her home, but also to start paying off the debt on the investment properties.

As Lisa's career progressed, and she was being promoted at work and literally taking over the world, Kate worked with her to buy more property to get her where she wants to be, not relying on anyone else for income, not relying on a state pension or super later in life and giving her — above all — choices and freedom. Having the option whether to work or not, whether to work part-time or not, whether to travel the world, see family in Europe, and enjoy life with some little luxuries here and there — that's all that it's about. Lisa's the ultimate female investor!

TO-DO LIST

- ☐ Make an obligation-free, no-cost appointment with a mortgage broker. Chat to them about your goals and have them assess what you can and can't borrow. This will start the conversation and you'll get some insights.

- ☐ Have a think about the size of loan that you're comfortable with and consider the repayment amounts that the broker will show you. You also need to know your own risk profile.

- ☐ Talk to a property-investment professional about timeframes and when it might be wise to apply for a pre-approval. Property and finance markets move and change all the time, so don't assume it's the same as it was last year.

- ☐ Start formulating your plan. It's always easier to build and gain momentum once you've actually started — which is what you've done — woo hoo, we say!

CHAPTER 3
WHEN TO BUY
The truth about property investment

You've got your finances sorted, you've got a plan of sorts, you've got mortgage pre-approval, you're good to go ... now what?

The truth is that successful property investment doesn't need to be difficult, nor does it need to be stressful or scary. Alas, though, many people stuff up their first property purchase, which is why so few people own more than one or two properties — contrary to some property haters out there who like to think it's because only 'rich (and probably male) people' can afford to build a portfolio!

We call 'rubbish' to that outdated line of thinking ... not that we're intending to teach you how to become a property gazillionaire. No, we will educate you on many of the things that you need to understand to help change your wealth, security and freedom using property investment.

You could buy one property or you could buy a dozen in your lifetime. Whatever works for you works for us, because we're not here to say there is a right or wrong way (well, within reason) to do any of this.

We're here to explain how it all works, so that you can make informed property decisions that will give you the best chance of creating financial independence in the future. And we're here to tell you about even the warty bits.

IT'S NOT ALL ROSES AND FLUFFY BUNNIES

Never before has it been easier to go down a real-estate rabbit hole online, has it? We call it 'property porn'! Those endless hours spent scrolling through property listings online, seduced by the snazzy pictures, the sexy styling and the (possibly) underquoted listing prices.

We've all been sucked into believing that what we see online is the perfect property for us — until we inspect it in real life and it's a first-class dump, or it sells at auction for $300 000 more than our budget.

> **HOT TIP**
>
> Property listings are a marketing tool designed to entice potential buyers. While they legally can't misrepresent a property to such a degree that it's misleading, it's vital to understand that online listings are simply advertising. Physical inspections by someone (it doesn't have to be you) are non-negotiable.

Generally speaking, many property investment spruikers will only tell you the bits that make their specific investment 'strategy' seem like an easy-breezy system that will make you oodles and oodles of money with very little effort from you at all. Well, that's just not correct, so here are our pros and cons of property investment.

THE GOOD BITS

Let's start with the good bits. Below are our pros of property investment.

LESS VOLATILE

Property can be less volatile than shares or other investments. Owning property helps people to improve their finances slowly, which is why we always advocate having a medium- to long-term mindset.

INCOME-EARNING

Investment properties earn rental income from tenants, which helps to repay the mortgage. There is the potential for passive income to occur once rent has risen to such a point (over time) that it covers the mortgage repayments as well as other associated property-related costs.

CAPITAL GROWTH

A strategically selected property increases in value over time, resulting in capital growth of the asset. This capital growth turns into equity, which can be recycled into more property and can improve your net worth, as well as help to generate passive income. Over a number of years, this capital growth compounds on itself, which is when the magic truly starts to begin.

POTENTIAL TO REDUCE TAX

No one should ever buy an investment property because of tax deductions or negative gearing. Sure, an investment property does provide the ability to potentially reduce your taxable income since you can offset the expenses against income earned, but it is capital growth that will ultimately make the biggest difference to your financial future. This is one of the reasons why we don't cover off on negative gearing in great detail.

NO TECHNICAL KNOWLEDGE REQUIRED

Now, again, this doesn't mean that there is a cookie-cutter approach that will suit everyone such as, 'There's a house, someone will want to live in it, so, you should buy it.' Rather, while due diligence and expertise is required to understand the best strategy for you, it's not an overly complex investment at the end of the day.

A TANGIBLE ASSET

While shares are an intangible asset, real estate is a tangible asset, meaning you can touch it, you can see it, and you can change it to improve its value if you so desire.

LIKED BY LENDERS

Without lenders, most people would never be able to increase their own wealth by using the power of other people's (lenders') money. Banks like lending on property due to its history of price growth, stability and tangibility. Indeed, lenders like it so much that for every one of your own dollars they will generally give you at least four of theirs. Winning!

CASH NOT ALWAYS NEEDED

As we explained in chapter 2, you will need some savings to put towards your first property purchase, but after that — as long as you buy wisely — you may not need to stump up much cash money ever again. That's because the capital growth in your property has produced equity, which lenders are usually happy for you to borrow against to allow you to purchase another property.

CONTROLLED BY YOU

There is nothing like an investment property for the control freaks out there! Owning it means you can decide what you want to do with it. You can renovate it — or not. You can hold it for decades and not sell it until you have retired. Or you can sell it to upgrade to a better property after one or two market cycles. Again, there is no right or wrong decision because the power is in your own hands. You are your own property boss.

> **HOT TIP**
>
> Many investment firms and gurus like to justify their existence and their exorbitant fees by overstating the complexity of all this. On the flip side, you'll get spruikers telling you there are 'no fees' to their so-called service. Yeah, right!
>
> Now don't get us wrong, there's a lot to think about and you shouldn't just blindly jump in.
>
> It's important, though, to consider how everyone is getting paid for helping you. Qualified professionals deserve to be paid for their advice as they are acting in your best interests — which is the opposite of spruikers who offer their services seemingly for 'no cost'.

BUYING COSTS TO CONSIDER

- ❏ Stamp duty (in Australia)

- ❏ Title transfer and mortgage registration fees

- ❏ Lenders mortgage insurance (if applicable)

- ❏ Conveyancing (legal fees)

- ❏ Building and pest inspection

- ❏ Loan establishment fees

- ❏ Buyer's agent and/or QPIA fee

SOME SELLING COSTS TO CONSIDER

- ❏ Pre-sale sprucing up, maintenance or renovations cost

- ❏ Real estate agent fees

- ❏ Marketing costs

- ❏ Conveyancing fees

- ❏ Bank or lender fees

- ❏ Capital gains tax

THE BAD BITS

Now that we've looked at pros, here are some pitfalls you should also be aware of.

NOT CHEAP TO START – OR FINISH

There is a sound reason why about 70 per cent of the Australian population owns property and the other 30 per cent do not. Mainly that's because some people won't earn enough to buy any type of property during their lifetime, which has been the way of the world for generations.

You do need that first deposit, plus extra funds to pay for buying costs. Likewise, there are expenses when selling, too, like sales commission and potential tax implications for investors. This is why we recommend always having a long-term ownership mindset, because it can be expensive on the way in and on the way out, too.

HOLDING COSTS

There will always be holding costs for property owners, whether it is a home or an investment property, which must be included in your budget. For first-time investors, the rent may not cover all of the property's expenses in the early days, so you need to have the cash flow to pay for these yourself.

INTEREST RATES

As we mentioned in chapter 2, interest rates can be volatile, which can impact your cash flow. One minute the rent may cover the repayments, and the next it may not because rates have been ramped up — and you can't just up the rent willy-nilly every time this happens. This is where it's important to understand whether fixed or variable rates might be best for you.

POSSIBLE VACANCY

All investors experience periods of vacancy during their journeys. Indeed, there is usually a period of time when your property is vacant between when one tenancy ends and the other one starts, because of the time it takes to change over tenancies, including exit reports and bond cleans. But your mortgage repayments are due come rain or shine, so you need to have extra funds to see you through these times.

NOT LIQUID

Real estate is an illiquid asset, which means that you generally can't sell it in a hurry if you get yourself in the financial poo, so to speak. Of course, this is one of the reasons why property makes such a reliable asset to invest in, but it also means that you can't just offload it at a moment's notice.

LOSS OF VALUE

Far too many women have been fooled by a spruiker's schtick and wound up buying an overpriced and rather crappy property in an inferior location — some mining locations, we're looking at you! They pay through the nose for something when the 'strong market' that was spruiked was always imaginary. The next thing you know, the property is worth less than they paid for it. This can also happen when a market softens quickly following its cycle peak.

NO SETTING AND FORGETTING

Some supposed property people advocate a 'strategy' that involves buying a property, engaging a property manager and then riding off into the distance on your thoroughbred horse without a backward glance. Ah, no ... Successful property investment involves decades of your time. Sure, most of the time it should actually be quite boring, but your longest relationship may well be with the properties that you buy.

UNEXPECTED EXPENSES

Any woman who buys real estate must have appropriate insurance to cover her investment, such as building and contents, as well as a landlord policy if you're an investor. But insurance doesn't cover everything that may go wrong with your property — or with your life, let's be honest — so sometimes you'll be slugged with a big-ticket expense that you weren't expecting, but that you will need to finance somehow.

NICOLA TELLS:

MY BIGGEST PROPERTY-INVESTMENT BLUNDER

Back in the early 2010s, I had one property to my name and thought I knew it all! I worked in the real estate sector but in hindsight, I didn't know anything about property-investment strategy.

I somehow crossed paths with a marketing person from a developer who was building a 'boutique' property in inner Brisbane. He was quite handsome. The next minute I had signed up to purchase a one-bedroom off-the-plan unit due for completion the following year — at least I got a more learned friend to guide me on selecting the best one-bedroom in the complex.

The building won awards but ended up being the first of many similar developments constructed in that suburb over the next five years.

Over the years, my unit has been vacant for a 10-week stretch, the rent is still below what it was when I bought it, and its value has only recently started to grow in any meaningful way — eight years after I settled on it.

It was a very expensive learning fee for me to pay in hindsight.

UNDERSTANDING MARKET CYCLES

One of the most important insights about property investment is that time 'in the market' always beats trying to 'time the market'.

If we had a dollar for every time that we've heard someone say, 'We're just going to wait for the market to cool down before buying', we'd have enough for another property deposit! This is a sign that someone is trying to time the market, which is nothing more than speculation and — let's face it — is a signal that they don't really get the basic concepts of property investment. This is because property markets generally move through cycles of good and not-so-good times over the years.

Whether you bought at the top or the bottom of the market won't really matter over the long term because significant capital growth is something that happens over decades and not months or years. We all know of someone who spent so long trying to time the market to 'perfection' that they ended up doing nothing at all, right? Another term for this is analysis paralysis!

We want you to buy the best property in the best location you can, when you can afford to do so, regardless of the market cycle, and then hold onto to it for as long as possible. If you do that once or twice, your financial future will be looking rosier than it would have been if you had done nothing at all as you vainly searched for the 'ideal' moment to pounce.

MARKET CYCLES

When it comes to market cycles, it's vital to understand:

- these phases may not happen in a particular order

- they may last a short or long time

- markets will often be at different phases at the same time.

This is because of a bunch of economic factors such as government policies, the availability of credit, global and socioeconomic factors, migration patterns and human psychology.

While it's important for you to understand market cycles and how they can impact your property-buying strategies, they should never be a reason not to proceed if you are in the position to do so.

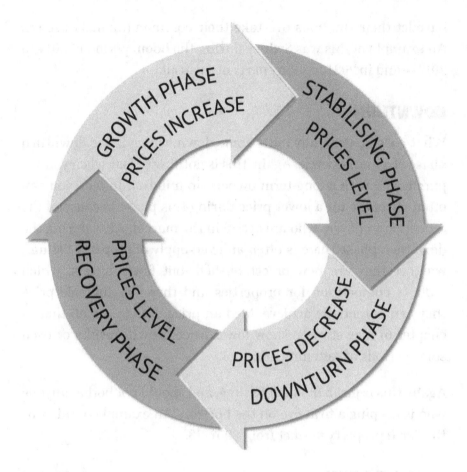

BOOM

When a property market is in the boom phase of the cycle, there is far more demand from buyers than there is supply of available property. Property prices are rising, and auction clearance rates are regularly at 80 to 90 per cent. The local economy is also usually firing on all cylinders. No one knows how long this phase will last — it could be months or years. While there are usually extreme levels of buyer demand in this phase, and low interest rates, that shouldn't stop you from purchasing a property if you are in the position to do so.

However, it's vital that you don't overpay because of the crazy prices that some people may be paying for properties because they have let their emotions overtake their common (financial) sense. An example of this was Sydney during the boom period of 2014 to 2017 — and in 2021 in many parts of Australia.

DOWNTURN

What goes up generally must come down, which is the downturn phase of a market cycle. Again, this is nothing to fear when you are purchasing with a long-term ownership mindset. In fact, you can often purchase for a lower price during this phase because of the reduction in buyers who are active in the market. Also, during the downturn phase there is often an oversupply of property listings, whether they are new or established, but fewer buyers, which reduces competition for properties and therefore the sale price they can potentially achieve. Median price data (more on that in chapter 6) may start to show lower price growth results or even some periods of softening prices.

Again, this is just a moment in time, and should not bother anyone who is keeping a firm eye on the horizon. An example of this was the Perth property market from 2007–13.

STABILISATION

The next phase of the market cycle is stabilisation, when not much happens for a while. This could be, and often is, years! This is when markets have roughly equal amounts of supply and demand and there is nothing overly spectacular happening in the local economy to drive prices higher.

This period can provide plenty of opportunities for buyers because there is usually not much competition for properties. But you should realise by now that the market cycle shouldn't dictate whether you purchase a property or not! An example of this was the Brisbane market for the best part of a decade after the global financial crisis (GFC) of 2007–08.

UPTURN

The final phase of the market cycle is the upturn when demand starts ramping up but supply often remains constrained — usually because of a reduction in new development as well as low confidence levels, more generally during the downturn or stabilisation phases. This is when you start to see buyers return to the market in increasing numbers with prices strengthening as a result. This phase can last months or years as well, before the boom times start all over again. An example of this hit most major markets in Australia and New Zealand at the tail end of 2020, when interest rates hit historic lows because of the economic fallout from the COVID-19 pandemic; demand was high, but listings remained relatively low.

WHY DOWNTURNS CAN BE GOOD AND BUBBLES CAN BE BAD

There is a more advanced technique that can help to improve your wealth-creation efforts.

Savvy property buyers can use market cycles to their advantage as long as they know what they are doing or have the expert assistance to help them do so.

One of the most successful investors of the past century is Warren Buffet, who famously coined the phrase: 'Be fearful when others are greedy, and greedy when others are fearful.'

This means buying counter or opposite to the masses, which is generally when the market is undergoing a downturn.

During the early days of the COVID-19 pandemic, when there was much fear and uncertainty, there was a temporary (as it turned out) lull in property markets. Some commentators were 'predicting' absurd price falls of 20 to 30 per cent when, in fact, property prices increased significantly over the year and kept going. Those investors who were able to purchase during the fallow period — and who understood the long-term fundamentals of property investment as a wealth-creation vehicle — probably achieved once-in-a-lifetime results over the short term.

However, you don't need something as serious as a pandemic to buy when others are not, as markets experience periods of softness all the time. Sometimes there are market downturns because of big global events like the GFC or the dotcom crash of 2000, but often it's just the normal mechanisms of a market cycle, including affordability issues after a period of strong property price growth.

For existing property owners, downturns are just a period of time during their journeys, but for purchasers they can provide more opportunities because of fewer active buyers in the market — as long as they have completed the necessary due diligence and research. The reality of the situation is that if you have bought, or own, a well-located property that is historically always in demand from buyers in that area, then downturns will likely have little impact on your property.

Just remember that during your property ownership journey, there will be periods of price growth, price stagnation and even price falls (on paper). What matters the most is that property has a proven history of price resilience and pressure over the medium to long term.

The most successful property investors are the ones who have the ability to ride out these market ups and downs because they know they are just temporary and the end result in years to come is the most important thing.

The term 'bubble' is bandied around in the media whenever a market boom is supposedly lasting too long, isn't it?

'Market bubble set to burst', the headlines often scream, which serves no purpose apart from scaring property owners and would-be buyers into making bad decisions such as selling too soon or not purchasing anything at all.

> **HOT TIP**
>
> **One technical definition of a property bubble bursting is when prices fall to _under_ what they were when the upturn cycle began. This usually only happens in speculative markets such as one-industry towns or in the new-unit sector, which is prone to oversupply.**

Bubbles are different to booming markets and generally don't happen very often, apart from in highly speculative situations where the herd mentality is pushing prices higher in locations where there aren't the economic fundamentals to back it up. That's why we advocate buying in areas that have diverse economies, as well as locations that are not going to be negatively impacted by oversupply, which we outline in detail in chapter 4.

WHY YOU MUST RESIST FOMO

We've all heard the term FOMO — fear of missing out — by now, haven't we? Of course, FOMO is not restricted to property, and can be applied to any decision-making that is motivated by emotion — that is, the fear that you're missing out on something good — rather than on sound judgement.

In markets that are booming, and even in the upturn phase, FOMO can result in people paying far too much for a property because their fear of missing out on the supposed future riches overrules any sensible decision-making. You can sometimes see this in action in auctions, when one person throws a single bid of hundreds of thousands of dollars on a property, to wipe the floor of all competition. Alas, that moment of victory may soon leave a bad taste in their mouth and a big hole in their financial future if the price they paid is drastically out of step with market reality.

KATE TELLS:

FOMO AT PLAY

I was once in the running to buy a three-bedroom property in the Sydney area for a client. It eventually sold for $130 000 over and above the guide price — yes, $130 000 more than they were expecting. Even the selling agent was surprised when offers hit the $750 000 mark when the most comparable sale was $715 000. Admittedly, the market was super-active and listing levels were low, but we'd guess there would have been some serious buyer's remorse happening on that one, and an even trickier time trying to secure finance from a bank at that price.

In property markets, FOMO can be driven by media hype as well as a type of market fever that makes no financial sense and actually reminds us of the Tulip Fever that happened way back in the seventeenth century. Indeed, the term, 'the madness of the crowds' is as relevant now as it was when it was coined way back then.

Spruikers in particular like to play on people's emotions, and especially FOMO, because their marketing collateral often relies on get-rich-quick schemes that will never work, such as buying houses for $1 and the like. Property buyers who become afflicted by FOMO are likely to find themselves overpaying for a property, which will result in lacklustre capital growth at best and financial ruin at worst.

Other times, though, fear can drive some people to sell a property too soon because of an 'imminent' market crash, or they may lose confidence in their plans and put off purchasing altogether. For women in particular this can be catastrophic as you may find it difficult to get a foothold in the market again, or you may miss out on years of potential capital growth, which can make a big difference to your financial freedom and security in the years to come.

Buying counter-cyclically is a sound investment strategy, but it does take courage and the support of experts. Strategic property investment should also never involve following the herd because there is supposed safety in numbers. This can be one of the biggest mistakes an investor can make.

Rather, you should ensure you have all of the information that you need to make a knowledgeable decision that suits you both personally and financially. Just because your brother, friend, aunty, or colleague is buying in a particular location, or a certain type of dwelling, does not mean it is the right property for you.

Have your own plan and do your own thing—and then take considered action without letting emotion muddy your decision.

'The best time to plant a tree was 20 years ago. The second-best time is now.'

—*Chinese proverb*

CASE STUDY: JENNIFER'S STORY

Kate was purchasing a property for her client Jennifer recently. Jennifer already had one investment property in her portfolio, but she had had no end of problems with the existing property. It had been vacant for quite some time, and since it settled she also had to pay out thousands of dollars in repairs that she hadn't budgeted for.

When Kate and Jennifer discussed how Jennifer had bought the property, they could whittle the mistakes down to two big ones caused by not using professionals to inspect the property for her.

Jennifer had a friend's sister who lived in the next town conduct the initial inspection.

She also didn't have a building and pest inspection done.

Using a property professional keeps you on track with an important property-investing basic—detaching personal needs, wants, and emotions from the purchase.

You're not buying a property for you, or your friend's sister, to live in forever; you're making an investment. A qualified building and pest inspector would have picked up on most of the defects that Jennifer had to rectify. If she had paid a few hundred dollars for the inspection, then at least she would have gone into the whole transaction with eyes wide open—and that is crucial.

TO-DO LIST

- [ ] Understand the pros and cons of property investment and don't let fear drive your decisions.

- [ ] Know your own risk profile, including what you are, and what you are not, comfortable with. Go in with your eyes wide open and remember there will always be risks to everything you do.

- [ ] Learn about market cycles. This is important so that you're at least aware of where property markets are at.

- [ ] Stay away from the herd. Forge your own path and try to resist FOMO.

- [ ] Recognise you're not buying for you. Forgetting this can be one of the biggest mistakes that people make.

CHAPTER 4
WHERE TO BUY
The lowdown on location

Rightio, ladies, this is where the rubber hits the road.

This chapter is so meaty it's like a buffet of property investment location intel! We suggest grabbing a cup of coffee or tea and finding a comfy spot before diving in.

There is much more to learn about most of this, but we don't want to produce a book that is 1000 pages long, either. You can head to the thefemaleinvestor.com.au and listen to our podcast to learn more!

RESEARCH, THEN RESEARCH SOME MORE

There are a number of different buying as well as investment strategies that might suit you best.

'Rentvesting' might be a solid idea for young women buying their first property because they can remain living and renting in their location of choice while investing in another area.

Likewise, borderless investing (buying in a location where you don't live; more on that later in this chapter) is a sound concept for anyone keen to create a portfolio and to make the most of different market cycles around the nation. For some women, though, their location options may be limited because they need to live in a certain area because of schools, employment, or custody reasons following relationship breakdown. These strategies still work for you because they will help you to determine the best areas to buy within your chosen location to maximise your chances of future capital growth.

Fundamentally, when it comes down to it, research and property screening are essential components of building a successful portfolio. There is no way around this in our opinion because we believe that meticulous due diligence and stringent property selection will also help to keep you, as an investor of property, safer as well as help to mitigate costly mistakes.

Even just covering off on half of our pointers will decrease the probability of buying a property lemon hugely, which can be one of the main reasons why women don't get past owning one property.

When it comes to location there are so many potential areas to consider that it can seem impossible to determine where may make a sound investment. Sure, there is plenty of research online as well as the regular release of property data, but do you understand any of it enough to make a thoroughly informed decision? Probably not.

As you saw in chapter 1, experts out there to assist include QPIAs, who can do all the hard work for you as well as make sure you are making the best investment decision possible.

UNDERSTANDING PROPERTY DATA

There is more property data available than ever before. You just need to jump online and do a few searches before you are neck-deep in statistics that are supposed to reveal the 'next big thing' for every woman who goes looking for it.

Alas, much of the data is old by the time that it is available because of how long it takes to collect it. For example, traditional median price statistics (which is the middle price of all properties sold in a particular location over a certain time period, such as a quarter or a year) is usually three months out of date by the time it's published. In rising or falling markets, this means that it really is not that relevant by the time you read it, but that's not to say that it doesn't have a place in your education.

On top of their propensity to be a bit 'musty' by the time they're released, data sets vary depending on which source you go to because of the different methodologies that they use. You can see how it can become confusing, right? And you can see why too many women get stuck in the analysis paralysis phase, can't you?

In our opinion, the most reputable data sources in Australia include CoreLogic, Domain, PriceFinder, SQM Research, Hotspotting, My Housing Market and Demand to Supply Ratio (DSR Data), as well as the Real Estate Institute in the state or territory in which you're buying.

When it comes to specific areas or suburbs for homebuyers and investors, there is also research that can help you determine which locations are superior to others (more on this in chapter 5, when we explore micro research concepts).

However, similar to any investment decision that you might make, it's important to assess and understand the data before proceeding. And with property investment, it's always about the numbers and the research — not your personal preferences or what you personally know or like, such as the suburb around the corner from where you currently live or where you grew up.

Various data sets and sources can be useful, depending on which stage of the buying process you are at. These include median dwelling prices, days on market, vacancy rates, gross rental yields, demographics, population growth projections and building approvals. Your expert team can do the heavy lifting for you, but it's worthwhile understanding what these statistics mean, which we have helpfully sprinkled through the book like knowledge confetti for you.

CHOOSE YOUR EXPERTS WISELY

We've all been exposed to well-meaning friends and family offering their version of property investment advice, haven't we?

Sometimes, it's from someone who may have lucked out by accidentally purchasing a property in a suburb set to boom, so they have become a self-styled investment guru.

Other times, it might be a friend who purchased in a supposed 'hotspot' but wound up financially worse off because of it. And, many times, our nearest and dearest might warn us about overextending ourselves — and sometimes they may be right.

But often it's because they don't have the same risk profile or they just don't understand the difference between good debt, which is a mortgage on a capital-growth and incoming-producing asset, and bad debt, such as personal loans and credit cards.

It's important to choose your experts wisely, including data sources and media stories, to ensure that you are learning from reputable sources. The same goes with agents who are on the selling side of a transaction, because their job is to secure a buyer as well as the best offer for their vendor's property — and not to provide purchasers with objective advice. Many buyers don't understand this fact well enough.

This means that during your property investment education you must seek out independent and unbiased advice from people and providers who don't have an agenda — and remember it's always about buying a property and not being sold one.

KATE TELLS:

LOCALS AND PROPERTY KNOW-HOW

I was once buying for a client in a strong capital-growth area in outer Brisbane. The client thought it would be 'prudent' to ask a friend who lived in Brisbane about that area and what they thought. The friend told my client to run a mile, the area was terrible, had a bad reputation and would never grow in value. After much debate and discussion and looking at the evidence, growth drivers that were coming to that area and the fact that I also knew the area well, the client decided to purchase a property there.

Just as well — it has since grown in value significantly, has never been vacant and is on track to be an awesome performer in my client's portfolio. The moral of the story is that local people do not always know anything about what drives property growth. They are too mired in their own prejudices. This happens all the time.

THE PRINCIPLES OF SUPPLY AND DEMAND

Before we move onto area selection, we need to tell you about the economic principle of supply and demand, which means that when there is high demand for something but low supply, this generally puts upward pressure on its price. Conversely, when there is low demand for something but high supply, then the opposite is true with prices generally not rising and even falling.

In a property context, this is the difference between a buyer's market and a seller's market:

◆ A high level of property supply and low demand is a buyer's market because there's so much stock to choose from, which can have a negative impact on capital growth.

◆ A low level of property supply and high demand is a seller's market because there is not much stock to choose from, which can have a positive impact on capital growth.

A successful property investor always considers supply and demand principles, including the prospects for future supply.

1. OVERSUPPLY ISSUES

When an area has oversupply issues, this can be caused by an abundance of vacant land available to be developed or currently undergoing development. This is common in new outer-ring city suburbs earmarked for master-planned communities, or inner-city locations where high-rise developments are plentiful because of advantageous local zoning. Often, these new properties are cookie-cutter in design and plentiful in number, which means that capital growth is likely to be subdued over the short to medium term.

2. UNDERSUPPLY ISSUES

When a location or a market has constrained levels of supply, this can be due to the fact that properties rarely come up for sale and when they do there is always strong buyer demand. This is common for houses in desirable inner- and middle-ring city suburbs, as well in locations that offer something special like river or ocean views. Likewise, these locations generally have very little land left to develop, which ignites property prices even further over time.

3. LOW BUYER DEMAND

When there is a lacklustre demand from buyers for property in a specific area, it is usually because of economic factors such as population decline, a poorly performing local economy — especially one solely reliant on one industry such as mining or tourism — or the market cycle is keeping most potential purchasers on the sidelines because of fear. Buyer demand can also be influenced by changing interest rates and lending policies.

4. HIGH BUYER DEMAND

High buyer demand can happen for various reasons including a growing population, increasing job opportunities in an area, a strong local economy and lifestyle attributes — things than attract residents to an area. An abundance of buyers can also be caused by changing interest rates and lending policies, which make it cheaper to borrow as well as repay a mortgage, such as during the second year of the COVID-19 pandemic.

Every property buyer and investor should have a basic understanding of the supply and demand metrics of the locations they are considering, to help them determine where and what to purchase. This can be done via tracking building approvals and other metrics for locations with lots of new property being constructed, but is more difficult to do in established suburbs.

> **HOT TIP**
>
> Just because an inner-city location has an oversupply of new units, which is dragging down prices for that type of property, doesn't mean that a house in the same location is not a savvy investment – its land component as well as dwelling type may be unique for that area.

There is a reason why the real estate catchphrase 'location, location, location' has stood the test of time. That's because location will always do the capital-growth heavy lifting of a property. You might be able to renovate or update a property, but you will never be able to change its location.

Likewise, buying any old house in any location over a superior unit in a better area doesn't necessarily mean the house will automatically appreciate in value significantly more. While it is land that appreciates in value, and the building itself will depreciate, if you have purchased a house in the wrong location, you might find that its value doesn't increase much at all because of a number of issues such as a new master-planned community nearby, a declining population, or its position on a busy road.

In essence, you should always try to buy a property in an area that has the best chance of being in strong demand from buyers in the future. This could be because of the desirability of the area, historic and continued low levels of supply, the potential to add value through renovation or subdivision, or it is simply the right dwelling type for the demographic of the people who want to buy there.

As we mentioned in our section on market cycles in chapter 3, supply and demand also fluctuates because of all manner of metrics, including the strength or weakness of a local economy. One small area of a city may be struggling with oversupply issues, while the rest of the market is doing quite nicely, thank you very much.

At the end of the day, if you just remember that strong demand but low supply is usually the precursor for capital growth, you will do much better than most!

AREA SELECTION

Now that you better understand the concepts of supply and demand as well as some of the property data sets out there, how do you go about selecting an area to buy property in?

For a female investor who wants to maximise her chances of stellar capital growth over the years ahead, it is always the area selection that will do most of the heavy lifting (excuse the masculine metaphor again — we really must think of a better one!).

For guidance on where to buy in a specified local area, we will outline some of the things to look for in chapter 5.

Most nations — and especially Australia — have different property markets scattered throughout their land mass that are quite distinct from each other. Of course, plenty of cities and towns have unique economies, but they also have diverse dwelling types and property markets that are often experiencing different phases of a market cycle at the same time — one city might be experiencing boom market conditions and one might be in a downturn.

> **HOT TIP**
>
> **Different areas do different things at different times and for different reasons. Not all property will perform the same in different locations.**

LOCATION MATTERS

You might be wondering, why is the area more important than the property for female investors? The answer is because if you get the location wrong, then your property will likely always produce underwhelming results.

For younger investors, sure, you have time on your side, but the property may only ever produce average, at best, capital-growth results because the location was wrong to start off with. For older investors, and especially for women re-entering the market after a relationship breakdown, then you may only have a decade or two before retirement, which means that you have no time to waste.

Remember that you're looking for long-term solid returns, and not speculating on a boom-and-bust market cycle! Your location selection must always be the top consideration — the area is your ace! You can buy a supposedly 'perfect' property, but if it is in a dud area then it simply won't grow in any meaningful way.

Likewise, never choose the property first, and never 'fall in love' with it, either. Instead, do your own research and work with experts to help determine which areas are likely to produce impressive results over the medium to long term because of their strong current, and future, fundamentals such as population growth, major-infrastructure investment and diverse economies.

You see, if you invest in the right area, even if the property itself is not perfect, then it will stand a fighting chance of growing in value over time. You can learn more about market conditions on thefemaleinvestor.com.au and via our podcast, too.

IS CITY OR COUNTRY BEST?

There are myriad locations that might make a sound investment area for you personally. This may be because of the price points of property there, or it could be because of the strong demand from buyers to live in that area.

The metrics that determine strong investment locations are many and varied, plus some areas might not suit you as investor because of your age, income or risk profile. That's why we keep harping on about staying away from anyone who suggests there is a 'one-size-fits-all' model for every single investor on the planet.

One of our friends in the industry once said about property investment, 'We're not talking about buying lollipops here,' and ain't that the truth! For many women, their home or their investment property will be the most money they spend on anything in their entire lives, which is why it's imperative that you don't rush into it, and you work with qualified experts who can help you.

Remember, it is always about the long-term economic fundamentals of a place, which can include metropolitan and regional areas. There is no rule book that says you must buy a house in Sydney, in Auckland, in London or Los Angeles to be deemed a successful property investor.

Rather, we believe property investment success is defined by buying the best you can, when you can, and holding on to it for as long as you can. If you can do that a few times, even better, but even if you can't, at the very least you will have something of your own that will help you create wealth, security and freedom through property. That is success in anyone's language!

KATE'S MYTH BUSTER

There's a popular belief out there that properties in regional areas don't grow in value in the same way that city-based properties do. This really is sheer nonsense. You can't set a blanket rule like that. As Nicola and I keep saying, each area has its own merits and deficiencies. Some regional towns and cities have capital growth that's superior to city suburbs. So, don't just dismiss them for no good reason. Do, however, be wary of something actually rural or remote.

5 AREA-SELECTION FUNDAMENTALS

Whether you wind up investing in a city or country area, a few fundamentals remain the same for female investors.

1. SUPPLY AND DEMAND

Consider the long-term supply-and-demand metrics of an area. For example, in rural and many regional locations, there is frequently a lot of land on which a lot of houses can be built. This means supply may outstrip demand and constrain future capital growth, whereas the opposite is usually true in parts of big and small cities, and major regional areas, depending on the location.

2. ACCESS TO AMENITIES

Whether someone is a potential tenant or buyer (and we always advocate purchasing a property that will appeal to future buyers rather than so-called 'investor stock' — yuck!), we humans generally want to have access to the same essential amenities such as jobs, schools, supermarkets, and lifestyle options like cafes and restaurants. If a location doesn't tick these boxes, it's probably not going to experience much in the way of property-price pressure because fewer people will want to live there.

3. FUTUREPROOF

Property markets in capital cities are futureproof because of the generations of people that continue to live there — although that doesn't mean that some of its submarkets (new inner-city units again) might not suffer from oversupply because of overzealous developers. For people to stay in a location for the long term, whether metro or not, it must be well serviced through organic and intrinsic growth factors such as a steadily rising population.

4. DOWNSIDES

Everywhere has its propensity for weather events that we can't control and that can, and do, wreak havoc on property. Just think of the floods in Queensland in 2011 as well as the earthquakes in Christchurch not long after. Of course, property prices in both of these markets are significantly higher than they were then, but you always must learn about a location's potential risks, including bushfires and cyclones, and make sure you are prepared for them with adequate insurance where possible.

5. REMOTENESS

We all know of a remote place where we dream about buying a holiday house, or perhaps have driven through over the years. Sure, it might be pretty and rather quaint with its one local shop that is also the petrol station, the post office and the library, but its property market is unlikely to do much at all. We believe there are many major regional locations that make excellent investment areas, but one-horse towns should be given a wide berth because they've been that way for a long time — and are set to stay that way, too.

KATE TELLS:

MINING-TOWN WOE

Many years ago, I was a novice investor who was drawn by the seemingly amazing cash flow and media hype of investing in a mining town. The pot of gold (probably mined locally) was just around the corner, it seemed, which totally clouded my judgement of assessing the area objectively.

So I bought into an area where the local economy was reliant on one industry — mining. But when the mining boom gasped its last breath and many workers were laid off and subsequently left town, I was left with plummeting rent and plunging value. There was way more supply than there was demand and the value of my property was soon less than the mortgage on it. Ouch.

This is why we advocate to only invest in areas with diverse economies, because even if one industry is experiencing tough times, its negative impact will not blow up the property market.

THE EXPERT'S GUIDE TO LOCATION

As part of your research into potential investment locations, you should start to uncover the demographics of people who live there as well as the current, and future, pipeline of major projects that are set to have a positive influence on the population and the area's livability.

Let's be honest — no-one likes living in a horrible house in a dodgy location, do they? Yet, we see uneducated investors buy terrible properties in horrible locations all the time — and then they wonder why it doesn't do much in terms of value uplift over the years!

They seem to have forgotten that while investors should never buy a property because they personally like it, they also should never buy something without any consideration of the people who will live there as tenants — and, most importantly, its potential future buyers, too.

Buying a good property in a great area will not only attract a higher weekly rent, but also better tenants who are likely to stay there for the long term and treat it as their home. In the future, there will also be more buyers prepared to pay good money for it, because you decided to invest in a good property rather than a shithouse one!

6 LOCATION METRICS TO UNDERSTAND

When researching potential investment locations, keep these six questions front-of-mind.

1. WHAT'S GOING ON THERE?

What are some of the current infrastructure projects underway and why are they important to an area's potential to thrive? Not all infrastructure is created equal — a new public art gallery or park might be very nice to frequent, but they won't create the significant jobs that a new hospital expansion will do. You should also only consider future major projects that have been funded, because there have been plenty of ventures that were stuck in the planning for decades and never went ahead at all. You can find out about major projects via local, state and federal government websites.

2. WHO LIVES THERE?

What are the demographics of the people who live there currently? Has it changed over recent years, and does it look set to keep evolving? This is especially the case for major regional areas that were once considered retiree enclaves but have gentrified because of an influx of new younger residents, usually because of housing affordability but also the ability to work from home. Is the population growing or declining? Clearly, a growing population is better than a falling one, but don't let population growth be the reason why you invest anywhere. Government data sources such as the Australian Bureau of Statistics are your best avenue to learn about area demographics.

3. WHERE DO THEY WANT TO LIVE?

Understanding the demographics of an area as well as population projections will help you assess current and future property demand. Again, each area usually has a specific dwelling type that is most in demand, so it's important that you understand what this is. You don't want to buy a small unit in an area that is predominantly families in need of three- to four-bedroom houses!

4. HOW WELL OFF ARE THEY?

The economic health of an area is crucial for it to grow sustainably. That's because when its residents feel confident about their financial situation, they are more likely to spend money on things like housing. During your location research, learn about the economic statistics and trends of an area, including employment rates, jobs growth, household income levels, gross regional product, and building approvals. Check that the local council is actively seeking to encourage and foster business growth. It's important to understand these metrics so you can determine the economic vibrancy of an area, which can be a precursor to capital growth. Much of this can be found via census data, but it is usually quite old by the time it is available. Local council websites and government sources are also more up-to-date research tools.

5. WHAT DO THEY DO FOR A LIVING?

Don't you hate it when someone you've just met asks you, 'What do you do for a living?' For those of us in the property and journalism game, well, our answers can see us talking to relative strangers about the next 'hotspot' or some media story they've recently read about the bubble bursting. There's no question that learning about the employment of the residents in a particular location will help you to assess the diversity of its economy. Again, locations that solely rely on one industry for their economic health — whether it be agriculture, mining, or tourism — are unlikely to make sound long-term investment locations.

6. WHAT'S THE SUPPLY SITUATION

Sorry to keep banging on about this one, but you must understand the current, and future, supply of properties destined for a location. To increase the probability of a maximum return on investment (ROI) as well as to minimise risk, your property must remain in as high demand as possible. So, gauge the current and upcoming supply of newly constructed properties in a respective area to be sure that oversupply is not present or imminent. You should also measure this against population growth and check out land availability — is it greenfield or brownfield? Greenfield is large blocks of land, like old farms, that can be turned into a new estate or master-planned community, while brownfield is from a former industrial site that can be developed, but may be contaminated. Expert advice is invaluable with this one.

> **HOT TIP**
>
> A diverse economy can still be stagnant temporarily and a one-industry town can be booming for periods of time. Ideally, you're looking for a location that has both—a broad range of booming industries in which people work.

BORDERLESS INVESTING

Borderless investing is buying in a different location or town to where you currently live.

This strategy is to maximise your chances of making the most of different market cycles, but also to create diversity in your portfolio. Rather than owning a property or two in your home location, you could invest in a property elsewhere to make the most of the market and economic conditions there as well.

Borderless investing has been growing in popularity for a number of years as more people learn about its potential advantages. However, that doesn't mean the strategy doesn't have some risks associated with it — they can be greater than buying closer to home for those women who haven't completed the required research before doing so. Here are some tips.

LOCATION FIRST

When any of us purchase a property to live in or as an investment, we rarely spend more than 10 or 15 minutes in it, do we? That's because open homes are designed to create competition and to push as many people as possible through in a short period of time, so the agent can move on to the next one. This is one of the reasons why the property itself is not as important as the location. So, if considering borderless investing, make sure you have done the necessary research on the location's economic fundamentals long before you have even narrowed down potential properties online.

PHYSICAL INSPECTION HURDLES

You must resist the urge to attempt to inspect every property yourself! Firstly, it will be very time-consuming and expensive to do this if the location is hundreds of kilometres away. We heard of one Sydney buyer who spent every weekend flying to the Sunshine Coast trying to purchase a property but wasn't successful — well, apart from the increase in their frequent flyer miles. Plus, unless you are a trained professional, do you even know what to look for and what are potential red flags during the inspection that you may have travelled for hours to attend?

IT'S NOT ABOUT YOU

Physical inspection of properties is one of the ways that they are sold to a buyer. That is, they are usually made to look as magnificent as possible through fresh paint, property styling, and even fresh flowers or cookies. All of these tools are used to engage with your emotions, so you start dreaming of owning or living in the property.

Of course, for investors, it should never be about what you personally like. Rather it is always about the property being the right type of dwelling for the demographics of the people who live there. A personal inspection can soon see you wearing rose-coloured glasses and making emotional decisions about purchasing it — always a bad idea.

EXPERT STRATEGY

We stand by borderless investing as a sound strategy for most investors, depending on their risk profiles. That said, it is not an overly risky strategy at all — as long as you have done your research or are working with qualified experts who can help you along the way. This book is about helping women understand all of the different facets of property investment, but we also are strong proponents of creating an expert team to help you achieve the best results possible.

CASE STUDY: SUSAN'S STORY

Susan is a single 26-year-old woman with a good steady job and a very encouraging and supportive family.

She has managed to save quite a sizeable cash deposit by continuing to live at home, reining in her spending, and being given a helping hand from her parents. Now, of course, we don't all get handouts from Mum and Dad, but she really has saved diligently over several years and also paid attention when her dad and brother talked about their property-investing journeys.

Cautious by nature, she did quite a lot of research about what she needed to do to get ahead, including reading books, listening to podcasts and speaking with finance professionals. Eventually she landed on Kate's doorstep. They discussed what she was looking for and what her budget and cash-flow needs were, and got straight to work.

Susan is now in possession of her first investment property. It's a bit of a fixer-upper, but she's looking forward to getting stuck into it. Plus, she has made a massive start on creating a secure financial future for herself. Go Susan!

TO-DO LIST

- [ ] Start researching and understanding different property data sets and sources.

- [ ] Always keep the supply-and-demand record spinning around in your head! Reread this section multiple times so you absorb and understand it all.

- [ ] Beware of 'friendly' property investment advice — only talk to qualified experts.

- [ ] Create a macro list of potential areas (metro or regional) that match your price criteria.

- [ ] Research the five area selection fundamentals to come up with a long list.

- [ ] Apply the six location metrics to create a short list of potential investment locations.

- [ ] Be open to not inspecting a property yourself and use expert help instead — this will open up the investment location possibilities big time.

CHAPTER 5

WHAT TO BUY

It's not just about the dwelling

By this stage of a female investor's research, you should have a fair idea of which areas have the best chance of helping to create your wealth, security and freedom through property. Now, let's move on to more micro investment factors, as well as the pros and cons of buying certain types of dwellings.

By now you know why location is such a buzz word in property investment circles — if you stuff up the location, then you can be doing yourself out of future capital growth and returns.

But area selection is not the end of the story — rather, it really is just the start! From that point on, you need to determine the best suburb or neighbourhood to invest in, and then preferably highlight the best streets within that location.

This level of research can be time-consuming and costly if you don't have ready access to the necessary datasets, but that doesn't mean that you should bypass it. Indeed, the opposite is true — this part of the process highlights that there are markets within markets and that the whole of an area is not the same.

So, how do you identify the superior locations to purchase within a specific suburb or neighbourhood?

5 SUBURB LOCATION METRICS TO UNDERSTAND

Often your selection will be dictated by your budget as well as your risk profile, but every female investor should understand these fundamentals before deciding on what to buy.

1. WHERE IS THE FUTURE DEMAND?

That is, where are there likely to be up-and-coming gentrification and demographic changes — as opposed to established blue-chip locations — that will probably have the most capital-growth potential? This is commonly called the sister suburb strategy — it's nice to finally have a female metaphor to use!

> **HOT TIP**
>
> A word about tenant demand, though. As an investor, while you are buying to rent to someone, you need to be able to sell to someone who wants to live there themselves in the future. Never forget this important fact!

2. WHAT ARE THE VACANCY RATES?

While residential vacancy rates don't tend to jump up and down quickly, it is important to understand any trends that show an imbalance in supply versus demand.

A vacancy rate is the number of rental properties (as a percentage of all rental properties) that are vacant in a particular location, such as a suburb or a city, at a particular time. The commonly accepted equilibrium point for rental markets is a vacancy rate of 3 per cent. When there is an oversupply of rental properties, then vacancy rates will be above this figure. If they have been above 3 per cent consistently for a while, it is probably best to avoid these dwelling types or locations. When vacancy rates are only 1 or 2 per cent, then those rental markets have an undersupply of rental properties. SQM Research provides the best publicly available research on these, and many other, important investment metrics.

While it is quite normal for vacancy rates to fluctuate a little, what you're looking for is a consistency of more demand than supply, which is common in many markets around the nation because of the strong demand from tenants to live in certain locations.

3. WHAT ABOUT AMENITIES?

Within your selected location, what and where are the amenities? Ideally there should be schools, cafes, parks, restaurants and shops nearby, but not necessarily next door for noise and traffic considerations.

The area should be well serviced and have some basic infrastructure in place. Walkability is desirable for many people, so will a tenant or a future buyer be able to walk to some of these places?

4. WHAT ABOUT TRANSPORT?

It's important to understand which modes of transport the local residents like to use, as well as where they live in relation to where they work.

If everyone drives, then it stands to reason that you need good parking. If lots of people catch the bus, then having a double lock-up garage is less important — but not unimportant because parking always adds a premium!

5. WHAT IS THE RENTER-OWNER RATIO?

This demographic can be one of the most vital when it comes to maximising your future returns. Why is that? It's because it's the future buyer of your property who will drive up its price, not the tenant who will rent it from you.

So, learn how many people own and rent within your chosen area, because this, too, can differ from suburb to suburb. Ideally, you want a 70–30 ratio of owners versus renters. Census data is often a good place to source this information.

Remember, it is always owner-occupier demand that will drive long-term and stable capital growth and not investors, who can be a fickler and more volatile bunch sometimes!

NEIGHBOURHOOD NITTY-GRITTY

As you can see, by this stage of your property-investment research you are narrowing down your selection from macro (area) to micro (street or neighbourhood).

Again, this will also be determined by what suits you financially now, and what is likely to keep suiting you in the years ahead. The best thing for you will differ from almost every other female investor, because of your age, your income, whether or not you have children, whether you are single, married, divorced, widowed, and your risk profile — to name just a few factors.

Just because your high-income-earning best friend decides to invest interstate does not mean that you should attempt to do the same. Conversely, if your goal is to own one investment property and hold that for the long term because that suits you the best, then your strategy may not correspondingly suit your bestie.

So, keeping with your own personal investment strategy, the next stage of your research is to learn everything you can about the property in your chosen neighbourhood.

9 NEIGHBOURHOOD KNOW-HOWS

Here are nine questions to keep in mind when narrowing down potential neighbourhoods.

1. IS IT ON A BUSY ROAD FOR THE AREA?
Try to stay away from significant traffic whenever possible. Reasons can include the noise, as well as kids playing in the street.

2. IS IT CLOSE TO A BUS ROUTE?
Access to a bus route is a positive as it is attractive for tenants and buyers. But you also don't want the bus stop right outside the front door.

3. WHAT IS THE SLOPE OF THE STREET AND LAND?
This can be important to know if there's drainage issues or when there's a lot of moisture or rainfall around. It will also be an indicator of whether retaining walls are prevalent in a street. Retaining walls literally hold land up. While we wouldn't necessarily avoid them altogether, they can be very costly to fix, depending on their purpose, height, size and construction materials.

4. IS THE PROPERTY ON THE HIGH OR THE LOW SIDE OF THE STREET?
Some local residents will be sensitive to whether a property is on the high or low side of the street. Again, this can be because of drainage, but also because of being overlooked or if there's a good or 'less good' view.

5. WHAT ABOUT ON-STREET PARKING?

Does the property have access to on-street parking for visitors? It's better if it does, depending on the location.

6. WHAT IS THE VIEW FROM THE STREET?

Views never go out of style, so if the property has desirable views, then that will always underpin its value in the years ahead.

7. HOW CLOSE IT IS TO POWERLINES?

Many areas still have aboveground powerlines, so you need to assess what impact this may have on the property. Properties close to powerlines will have large easements on them, affecting value and desirability. Make sure powerlines are out of sight.

8. IS IT IN A FLOOD OR BUSHFIRE ZONE?

The property may be negatively impacted by these zonings, which can increase insurance premiums, and reduce value and desirability.

9. ARE THERE ANY OTHER WARTY BITS?

Are there any weird location-specific bits and pieces that will put off tenants and buyers? For example, manufacturing smells or daily car-parking problems from commuters.

HOT TIP

Investors from big cities can often put too much emphasis on proximity to public transport. In Sydney and Melbourne, it can be desirable to live close to a train station or on a busy bus route. Don't assume that's the case everywhere! You need to know how people get around, where they live and work, and whether anyone actually uses local transport. There is no point being next to a train station that no one uses — in fact, it may actually be considered detrimental to a property's value because of the constant noise.

DWELLING TYPE PROS AND CONS

To increase the probability of maximising your ROI and minimising risk, your property must remain in high demand as much as possible. This means that you must consider who you are buying for and why this matters when you select a dwelling.

Do you know who is going to rent your property? Do you understand who is likely to buy it when you sell it in many years to come? Don't forget what we said in chapter 3 — you're not buying for you.

If you don't understand these metrics, then you are not ready to put an offer on a property. Fundamentally, investors must buy a property that is in the most demand from the demographics of the people who live there now, and who will live there in the future. Again, that means not buying a unit in an area where 80 per cent of people are purchasing freestanding houses on large blocks of land. This will always reduce the potential future buyers for your property.

If your budget won't allow you to buy a house in a location where houses are the most popular, you should consider other locations where you can afford to do so.

Alternatively, purchase a superior unit in an area where these properties are the dwelling type of choice for buyers (such as in certain suburbs closer to city centres or locations with desirable attributes like water views).

The next section will outline the pros and cons of different dwelling types, but always remember that any of these might be the best option for you as an investor. Plus, we're not saying one type of dwelling is better than the other, but you need to be aware of all the pros and cons to make an informed decision.

Finally, when we say established, we mean any property that was constructed at least two to three years ago.

HOT TIP

Land value rises, building value declines

Generally speaking, and again depending on a number of variables, land rises in value, but buildings depreciate in value. This is why house prices are higher than units — because of the larger land component of a house. Over time, capital growth is usually higher for houses than units — but not always. However, the beauty of the Australian tax system is that it allows you to offset your paper loss of the depreciating value of the building, which can improve cash flow during your period of ownership. The reality is when you purchase a house on decent land, the land will generally rise in value, but not every block of land everywhere will rise in value. It all comes down to supply and demand!

ESTABLISHED HOUSES

PROS

♦ Buyers are less likely to be surprised by anything untoward — the house has been in the same spot over many years or decades.

♦ Less likely to experience downturn in value due to oversupply — established properties are generally located in fully built-up locations.

♦ More likely to have infrastructure and lifestyle features in place — it is probably in an established area or suburb.

♦ Less likely to experience higher periods of tenant vacancy — it's usually located in an area with lower likelihood of oversupply of similar properties. The reality is when you purchase a house on a reasonable land size for the area that you're buying in, the land will generally rise in value. However, if you are one of 5000 blocks that all come on the market at the same time and there is a consistently high amount of supply and not enough demand to soak it all up, then your block will not grow in value. It all comes down to supply and demand! Not every block of land everywhere will rise in value.

◆ Less likely to have big maintenance items — the previous owners have had the headache of owning the property from new. They've fixed all the 'brand new property' building and fixture issues. The same can't be said for much older houses, which can still make great investments because of their scarcity factor, but you need to be able to afford the maintenance and repairs.

◆ Not as susceptible to nasty spruikers of property — there's nothing in it for them when 'selling' established property. They focus almost exclusively on brand new as they make a fortune in commissions.

◆ The property exists already — you know exactly what you are getting and can be totally confident of the finished product.

◆ No waiting for the property to be finished — you can move a tenant in right away once it's yours.

CONS

◆ Not as many government incentives — with regard to things like stamp duty, you're generally paying full whack.

◆ May be more susceptible to maintenance issues — depending on its age and the quality of the build, and after a certain period of time there's no building warranty in place for property.

- May have to replace some internal fixtures and fittings — replacing things like paint and carpets can add to the buy-in price.

- May have to replace or fix some appliances — water heaters, air conditioners, ovens and dishwashers can add to the buy-in price.

- Possibly not as appealing as brand new — tenants do like to live in a nice new property, but owner occupiers do love an established house!

- Possibly has local suburb 'stigma' attached — this tends not to happen in a brand-new area as it's too new to have got a bad rep.

ESTABLISHED TOWNHOUSES, DUPLEXES, UNITS

PROS

- Affordability — often the main driver for investors who buy units. Median unit prices are noticeably lower than median house prices in every capital city in Australia.

- Investment opportunity — as long as you get your location and dwelling selection right, buying an established unit or townhouse can make the difference between being able to get into the market or not.

- Superior location — unique units (such as Art Deco) in superior locations generally stand a better chance of value uplift than second-rate houses in inferior areas.

- Lower maintenance — units are arguably easier and cheaper to maintain than houses.

- Higher rental yield — due to lower purchase prices, a higher gross rental yield is common with units and townhouses compared to houses. However, this can be a false friend as cash flow will never make anyone wealthy.

- Location — there is a trend for town planners to focus on increased density in established areas, close to existing infrastructure and employment. Plus, you can often purchase a unit in a better location where you couldn't afford to buy a house.

- Shared risks and costs — no one likes to pay body corporate or owners corporation fees, but these funds do mean that external property-related expenses come out of existing reserves rather than your own bank account.

CONS

- Higher overall holding costs — the strata fees we mentioned earlier can be a big expense for owners and can eat into your cash flow. The more bling in the block (think pools, lifts, rooftop gardens and the like, which are classed as common property), then the higher the fees.

- Joint decision-making — all major decisions are made by the collective group of owners, which can sometimes be good and sometimes be bad, but generally it means you have less control over your unit than you would if you owned a house.

- Little point of difference — it can be tricky to create significant differences to other units in the complex, even after renovations.

- Oversupply issues — again, the major problem with units in particular is their susceptibility to oversupply, which can drag down the prices of all units (including established) for a significant period of time.

- Less demand — attached dwellings generally have less demand from buyers, depending on the location.

NEW PROPERTY

PROS

- Increased tax-effectiveness — the newer the property, the greater the tax deductions via depreciation. New property can notably improve cash flow and can effectively be more affordable for an investor for this reason.

- Lower maintenance — no prior wear and tear, which reduces the need for ongoing maintenance or the replacement of any furnishings or fittings for many years.

- Enhanced tenant and resale appeal — appeal of newly constructed property can provide an edge when seeking tenants or a future buyer.

- Stamp duty savings — in Australia there are often concessions for people (and especially first-time buyers) constructing a new property, which can reduce the funds you need to purchase.

- Building protection — newly constructed properties generally have a builder's warranty period that provides homebuyers and investors with some safeguards in the event of significant structural or other building issues.

CONS

◆ Premium price — paying a premium for brand new versus a
lower price for something established, potentially around the
corner, may have an impact on future capital growth prospects.

◆ Where's the property? — the property often doesn't exist yet,
but you're tying up large amounts of cash or equity in an
asset that has yet to be built.

◆ There's nothing but fields around — new houses in particular
are also often located in a developing area with little
infrastructure in place such as not enough roads, schools,
shops, hospitals — these can be quite a drive away and take
longer than expected to be constructed.

◆ Building risks — it can be more susceptible to structural
building issues than a more established one that's already
been sitting in the same spot for 20-some years.

◆ Supply problems — supply is the enemy of capital growth.
Of course, new house and unit developments are needed
as populations grow, but additional supply reduces buyer
competition which, in turn, impacts capital growth.

◆ Increased vacancy — likewise, when there is additional
supply of new dwellings, then tenants have more to choose
from, which can result in increased vacancy periods that
may affect your ability to hold for the long term.

◆ Spruiker alert — new property can be the domain of some
spruikers, who are usually selling on behalf of developers
for big commissions that they don't disclose to you, but who
come across to buyers as their new best friends.

◆ Depreciation is nice, but — the ability to maximise
depreciation benefits on a new property is a nice-to-have,

but remember that you are investing for capital growth and never for tax savings.

♦ Beware rental guarantees — these are guarantees paid by the developer that are designed to put an investor's mind at ease but are really an indication that the property may struggle to attract a tenant for some time. Run a mile! These guarantees are also often built into the price you're paying for the property, so it is far from a free handout. No new property or unit should need a rental guarantee if it is the right investment in the right location.

♦ Finance hurdles — securing finance for a new home can also be more complex, because part of the loan is likely to be a construction loan, which will be drawn down during building when the lender is satisfied specified works have been completed.

WORD OF WARNING

Most people living in a city in Australia will be aware of the increasing number of major structural building issues that are coming to light in newer high-rise-unit developments. In some cases, residents are being forced to vacate the buildings for several months and even years while the issues are being fixed, lawyers are engaged, litigation is commenced and compensation is sought. Be aware of the pros and cons of new property and complete adequate due diligence before purchase — this is an absolute non-negotiable for all of our female investors. Trust us when we say that it's always better to walk away from a deal having spent a few hundred dollars on expert and quality-inspection reports than have to fork out hundreds of thousands of dollars a year later because of defects that no one wants to fix. Not to mention the stigma then assigned to that building, which will affect your future capital growth.

A FEW WORDS ABOUT VACANT LAND

You might have noticed that we haven't outlined the pros and cons of buying vacant land and that's because we don't believe it is for the beginner investor. You really need to do some heavy due diligence when purchasing a block of vacant land (and we mean a vacant block within an existing suburb and not a master-planned community).

You may need to negotiate with council to rezone for development, plus there are substantial upfront costs, and extensive lag times before you make any income after constructing a property on it. Of course, we're not saying vacant land is no good, it's just a different level of investing, and not what this book is about.

PROPERTY PECULIARS

By this stage, you should have a fair idea of the property that you are keen to purchase in a particular location — or are working with qualified experts to help you work that out.

The most important thing to keep in mind from this moment on is whether the property appeals to the local residents. This will help maximise your ROI in the future as well as minimise the potential risks.

Does it have what they're looking for? What are the must-haves and nice-to-haves? What can you compromise on and what can you not?

Also, make sure you view the online photos with a grain of salt because they may have been edited to within an inch of their lives (although not to the point of false and misleading) or they could actually have been taken a number of years ago.

17 PROPERTY PECULIARS

There are a variety of property metrics (or peculiars) that you must also start to understand so you know exactly what you are purchasing as well as whether there are any additional pros and cons you need to consider that could cost you, or make you, money.

1. WHAT IS ITS CONSTRUCTION?

What age is the property and what materials was it constructed from? Different materials have different maintenance costs attached. Some materials, such as asbestos, are expensive to remove, while weatherboard can cost a lot more in upkeep over the years. Likewise, what is the roof material? Is it tiled or tin and what condition is it in?

2. WHAT IS THE LAND SIZE?

Is the property on a land size that is in demand in the location? If it's a unit, does it have an above-average land component attached to it?

3. IF IT'S A UNIT, WHAT IS THE SIZE OF THE COMPLEX?

Smaller is better. What floor is it located on? Units on higher floors generally have better resale prices because of the potential for superior views and their increased distance from street noise.

4. ARE THERE ANY RETAINING WALLS?

There's a difference between simple low garden-bed retainers and two-metre-high wooden retaining walls that are holding up the property next door. Know what you're dealing with and the associated maintenance costs.

5. ARE THERE ANY ZERO BOUNDARY WALLS?

A zero boundary refers to a structure being built up to or very near the edge of the boundary line of the owned land. You need to check whether there is any part of the property or the building that you can't get to easily because it's right on the boundary line. Sometimes a wall or side of a house is set right along this and if there is a maintenance issue it means you'll need to access the neighbour's property to get to it. It's not a deal-breaker, but this can be awkward, so just be aware.

6. WHAT IS THE PROPERTY'S ASPECT OR ORIENTATION?

In some states, local residents don't like a property, the yard or rooms within the property to be facing in a certain direction; for example, if it gets the full blast of the Queensland western sun in the afternoons. Know which way the property is facing and whether this is positive or negative.

7. WHAT IS THE TYPE OF TITLE?

Is it strata? Torrens? Community? Each of these is a type of title that defines the ownership rights for that dwelling.

Torrens title simply means the purchaser owns the land and building. This can also be known as 'freehold'.

Strata title simply means that there are multiple owners of properties on one piece of land where all owners are responsible for the areas that are shared, known as 'common areas'.

Strata and community title generally refer to units or townhouses, with some more titles more common in some parts of the country than others. Torrens title would generally refer to most freestanding houses.

Your accountant or legal team member will be able to provide more advice about this one. This is massively important when it comes to purchasing a property and could take a whole chapter by itself. However, we recommend that you always find out what title the property has before you purchase or make an offer. Some title types are not common in an area and will make a property harder to sell than something that is more typical. For example, a freestanding four-bedroom, two-bathroom house on 500 square metres of land could still be strata titled for a variety of reasons and this will hugely affect your potential to sell it if this is unusual in that area.

8. WHAT IS THE OVERALL CONDITION OF THE PROPERTY?

Make sure you check the condition of the paint, carpets and roofing; the state of the exterior, the yard and so on, to see if you may need extra funds to improve these elements before it can be rented out.

9. WHAT IS THE FLOOR PLAN?

How many bedrooms, bathrooms, living areas and laundry spaces does it have? Is that the right number for the type of people who want to live in the area?

10. WHAT ARE THE PROPERTY'S FACILITIES?

Does it have off-street parking or access to on-street parking? What about a double or single lock-up garage? This can be particularly valuable in inner-city areas.

11. WHAT ARE ITS FIXTURES AND FITTINGS?

Does it have fly and security screens? What about ceiling fans or air-conditioning units? What type of flooring does it have and what is its condition? The same goes for the kitchen appliances such as cooktops and dishwashers. You must check the age and condition of all of these to determine whether you may need to update or replace them to secure a tenant.

12. WHAT IS THE OUTDOORS LIKE?

Is there a balcony or covered patio? Is the backyard in good condition or does it need serious landscaping to bring it up to scratch? What sort of outdoor attributes are most in-demand in the area and does this property fit the bill?

13. WHAT IS THE PET POLICY?

For units and townhouses, you must understand the strata bylaws, including the pet policy. It's becoming increasingly important (and rightly so, if you ask us) that tenants can have their furry friends living with them, which can also mean they will rent your property for a longer period of time, too.

14. WHAT ARE THE UNIT FACILITIES?

Many newer unit developments have a plethora of high-end facilities that draw in would-be buyers and are attractive to tenants. The reality of the situation is that these cost money to maintain, which will come from your body corporate fees and, fundamentally, your own back pocket.

15. ARE THERE ANY ADDITIONS?

Has the house had any alterations or additions? If it does, do they have the necessary building approvals for them or are they even legal?

16. ARE THERE BUILDING OR PEST PROBLEMS?

Every buyer should have a building and pest inspection for a property, but you can also ask the agent whether there are any issues upfront. If they are aware of any major issues (or material facts) about the property, they are legally required to tell you about them. Check if there any existing pest-management systems in place.

17. ARE THERE ANY FEATURES THAT ARE NOT PART OF THE SALE?

It's not uncommon for a property to be stripped of certain things, such as curtains or blinds, before settlement. There is nothing wrong with this happening as they may have never been part of the sale to start off with; however, you must understand what is included in the contract of sale and what is not, so you don't get any nasty surprises once you officially own it.

***

As you can see, there are many things that you need to understand — and these are just a few — before you purchase a particular property, including always considering how it compares with the suburb average and what local residents want in a home, whether they are buyers or tenants. Make sure that it ticks enough boxes for that location specifically!

> **HOT TIP**
>
> ## Ask yourself the 'pink kitchen cupboard' question
>
> OK, so you've found a great-looking property, or so you think. You scroll through the pictures online and come to the all-important kitchen. Proudly shown is a great kitchen with pink cabinetry, and you recoil in horror. You hate pink, you loathe pink, you can't stand the thought of buying a house with a pink kitchen. To be blunt, what you think doesn't matter. If your property research tells you that all the local people love pink kitchens, then that's what you buy. Of course, this isn't a real scenario, but the moral of the story is never, ever assume that what you like and want is the same as what those local people want. The same goes for things like the number of bedrooms, land size, floor plans, proximity to trains and so on. For investors, buy what's in demand locally, whether you like it or not, because you're probably never going to live there!

BUT HOW DO YOU FIND OUT ABOUT ALL THIS STUFF?

Your brain is probably hurting a bit by now, right? Plus, you are probably starting to understand why strategic property investment is a bit trickier than buying any old property in any old place and hoping for the best.

As we've outlined, there is a bunch of property data that can assist you with determining the best locations and the ideal properties to buy, plus plenty of experts out there to help you as well. But, if you're going it alone, you will need to dig deeper than just what is publicly available online. In fact, you probably should pick up the phone, or pound the pavement if you can, and have a chat to the people who most likely are the local experts on all manner of things.

The local shopkeepers, sporting clubs and councils can be a useful source of information, and they often love to chat about their neighbourhoods as well! The local council town planner also can provide you with lots of intel on what is happening in the area when it comes to developments or any upcoming zoning changes.

For investors, and especially borderless ones, sometimes working with a local property manager can assist with important local knowledge such as which properties are the most in demand from tenants. Property managers are also great at inspecting properties, for obvious reasons, if you are unable to attend yourself.

While we have probably given selling agents a hard time so far (we apologise for that because we know many and they are our friends), they can provide plenty of answers to your questions about a local property market and especially the type of real estate that buyers desire the most.

KATE TELLS:

INFORMATION GOLD

I do a lot of area research as part of my job. Once I was chatting to a town planner in a council in a major regional town in Victoria and I totally made this guy my new best friend. He was more than happy to tell me anything and everything I wanted to know about the town. The best part was that after a while I started asking him some quite personal questions. Because he was also a newly arrived local resident, he shared some stories with me about where the kids went to school, what people liked to do for fun, where everyone does their shopping, what the council was planning ... real local information gold that helped me determine some great location hotspots within that town.

When you have completed all the research that you possibly can, then you must consider what does and doesn't need to be done at the property, and whether you have the funds to do these if needed. However, always remember that you will never find a property that ticks every single box. It's about buying the best property that you can considering all of the elements we have outlined so far.

By completing the necessary checklists, you will know whether:

◆ it is in the right location

◆ it has the basic must-haves

◆ you can afford it

◆ it's 'good enough' for that specified location.

Well, then, it's finally time to hit the calculator to do a detailed cash-flow analysis. That is, what are the total costs to own the property versus the rent that it will earn — can you afford to fund any cash-flow shortfall? Then you should appraise its value by using recent — as in within the past few weeks or months, depending on market conditions — comparable sales, so you can best determine the price of your offer for the property.

This is when things can start to get really interesting. Hang on to your hats, ladies!

CASE STUDY: ELAINE'S STORY

Elaine had wanted to buy investment properties for many years and had been held back for a number of reasons. She bought her first apartment to live in when she was 24, encouraged and inspired by her mum, a single mother, who herself had bought her first place when she was 20.

She had a dream to purchase a property every year, save the deposit, and keep purchasing. An eight-year relationship followed, and her partner was reluctant to invest because his own parents had made some poor financial decisions, which made him a bit gun-shy. But Elaine never lost her enthusiasm and when that relationship broke down, she got down to business researching and planning the expansion of her property portfolio.

Another relationship came along, which put things on hold again, but a couple of years later she was up and running and purchasing. Six investment properties and her own new home to live in later, Elaine and her little boy are set for life. Her dream was growing a property portfolio that gave her security and financial freedom, and above all, choices for herself and her young son. She has achieved all of that and more. Elaine, we are all so proud of you!

TO-DO LIST

- [ ] Read all those pros and cons again — know what you're comfortable getting into. This really is so important.

- [ ] Get organised and get your checklists ready. Understand the questions you're answering here and why they're important.

- [ ] Go through your checklists and find the sources of information.

- [ ] Check your five suburb metrics.

- [ ] Test your nine neighbourhood know-hows.

- [ ] Prove your 17 property peculiars.

- [ ] Drill down into the essential must-haves and nice-to-haves for each area that you're looking in. Be clear on what you can and can't compromise on.

- [ ] Determine the price you are prepared to offer.

CHAPTER 6

HOW TO BUY

Negotiate like you mean it

Did you know that some of the wealthiest people in the world are top-notch negotiators?

The most successful property investors are expert negotiators, whereas, many deals fall over because the buyer or the seller isn't being realistic about the price that they are prepared to offer or accept. This is especially the case in rising or booming market conditions because of the disconnect between what a seller is prepared to sell their property for and what a buyer is prepared to pay!

Just think of that old real-estate saying about how a seller thinks their property is a castle but the buyer views it as a rundown shack, and you can probably best understand what we're talking about.

This is the moment when emotions can cause both parties to make silly decisions, such as a buyer paying too much for a property or a seller refusing a strong offer because they are holding out for a number that is unrealistic. Most vendors engage a sales agent to represent them during the process, which means that buyers are often trying to negotiate with someone who does this every day of the week. Of course, this can put them at a disadvantage from the get-go.

People who opt to work with buyer's agents can neutralise this situation because they also have a professional negotiator on their team — who may have also bought a few properties for their clients from that particular agent in the past, too. There is a reason why so many books are written about negotiating, because it is a skill that must be learned and practised time and time again.

Most buyers will only purchase property a few times in their lives, which means that they are never likely to have the same skill levels as a professional who does it all the time. Now, that doesn't mean that you can't create a strong negotiating position for yourself if you're going it alone. It's just that you must have completed the necessary due diligence beforehand to give yourself the best shot possible.

DOES THE BUY-IN PRICE MATTER?

There is another common saying in the property investment space, which is 'you make money when you buy'. This is because if you overpay for a property, it can have a detrimental impact on your cash flow over the short to medium term.

Remember in chapter 2 when we wrote about the importance of knowing your budget? Well, this is the moment when it is the most critical. If your budget for a property is $700000 but you wind up paying $800000 because you let your heart rule your head, what ramifications will that have?

Firstly, you will probably have to pay a bigger deposit, or use more equity from an existing property. However, it will mean that your mortgage repayments are going to be higher as well, which can squeeze your cash flow. When you are assessing what price to offer for a property, always remember your cash-flow position after settlement, so you do not end up paying too much for it.

In hot market conditions, it can be difficult to determine the market value of a property, and therefore some buyers may end up paying more than they thought they should. But if they can finance the higher amount as well as the additional strain on their cash flow, it may not be a major problem for them. For female investors and many property buyers, though, if you pay too much and then find yourself unable to keep up with your mortgage repayments, especially if interest rates increase, then you may be left in a precarious financial position.

For investors, you must also assess what the market rent is likely to be for the property before making an offer. Sometimes the property is currently leased so you might presume that the rent the tenant is paying is the market price, but this isn't always the case, and especially for long-term tenants who may have been paying under market value for a while because of their long tenure.

> **HOT TIP**
>
> A simple and quick but invaluable research trick: have a look at the rental listings of a property website and check out some current properties listed for rent that are similar to the one you're going to make an offer on. This will give you a rough idea of what rent to expect on your new investment property and, if the property is already tenanted, whether the current tenant is paying a fair market rent for that property.

Median rent and median yield data are publicly available, but don't rely solely on these statistics. There are so many variables between properties. For example, a three-bedroom house that is in 'original condition' will not achieve the same rent as one in the same suburb that has been renovated to a high level. Likewise, a two-bedroom unit with river views will achieve a higher rent than a two-bedroom apartment on a busy road in the same area.

It's a good idea to speak with local property managers from agencies not involved in the sale to understand the market rent for the property.

WHAT ARE RECENT SALES OF SIMILAR PROPERTIES?

The price a property is listed for sale should be within a reasonable estimate of what it is likely to sell for ... should be!

Sometimes, the sale price can be far above the list price because of the market conditions as well as buyer competition, especially at auction. In fast-moving markets, prices can be rising so quickly that sales from a few months ago are already 'old news', which is why buyers can struggle to assess what offer to make on a property.

Again, median prices at suburb level are really just an indication of the middle sale price of properties in an area, which can help you determine which locations are within your budget. Median prices are also usually quite dated by the time they are published, as we've mentioned previously. Make sure you understand the recent sale prices of comparable properties in the local area, which you can learn from sold statistics online or by reaching out to local sales agents.

It's vital to only use sales that are similar to the property you are hoping to buy, which means comparable quality, land size, number of bedrooms, bathrooms and the like, because otherwise you are not comparing apples with apples.

DON'T TAKE THE BAIT

Bait pricing is illegal in most states. It is an unethical advertising technique that involves luring potential buyers in with the promise of a lower sale price than has actually been agreed with the seller of the property. It is designed to attract more buyers than can actually afford the property, create a false sense of demand, have buyers fall in love with it, and drive the price up. But all the while the sales agent knows that half the interested buyers cannot afford the property. While this practice is, as we say, illegal in many states, it still runs rampant and is even more reason to make sure that you know what a property's value actually is and don't rely solely on the guide price given by a sales agent.

HOW ARE PROPERTIES BEING SOLD?

Regardless of market conditions, properties in some locations are predominantly sold by private treaty, or they may be sold by auction.

Private treaty is when a property is listed for sale and buyers submit an offer — this is generally the most common type of sale in Australia and New Zealand. This sales method can be frustrating, though, as you don't usually know what other offers are being made on a property. When there are multiple buyers keen on a property, then you should be given the opportunity to put forward your best and final offer, always keeping in mind your ideal buy-in price, regardless of how much competition there is for the property.

Auctions are becoming more popular in every market and are usually the dominant sales method for properties that will be in hot demand from buyers because of their scarcity. If you are going to purchase in a location where auctions are the most common, you should educate yourself on the process and perhaps try to attend a few so you can see how they are conducted.

Auctions are designed to increase competition for properties, but that doesn't mean that they are something to be feared — rather, it can be the most transparent way to buy a property as you can literally see and hear what the other buyers are bidding. There are usually special conditions attached to auctions, such as being cash unconditional contracts, which you will need to understand and prepare for (with loan pre-approval for example) for the local jurisdiction of the property.

Some of the data to understand to help guide you includes private treaty sale numbers and auction clearance rates. When auction clearance rates are high (that is, the percentage of properties successfully sold under the hammer, which can vary depending on the location), this means that the market is generally in the seller's favour.

A final word on the Holy Grail of property investment — off-market sales. These are properties that a sales agent will try to sell via their networks, often because the vendor doesn't want the hassle of a private treaty or auction campaign. Depending on the market conditions, off-market sales can be quite prevalent or very thin on the ground.

When market conditions are soft, off-market sales are usually more common because the opportunity to purchase without competition is valuable to buyers. However, they are less common when markets are booming, because there is guaranteed strong buyer demand to drive the price up.

The thing about off-market sales is that they are pretty much an industry secret — that is, a regular buyer is very unlikely to ever learn about them because they don't have strong relationships with local agents. Buyer's agents and QPIAs, on the other hand, are often the first people that a sales agent calls with an off-market opportunity because they know them, they trust them, and they also understand that their clients are financially ready to purchase — win, win, win all round!

DUTCH AUCTIONS

Also sometimes called *silent auctions*, these can be tricky to navigate. They are a bit of a mash-up between a private treaty sale and an auction. It's where agents personally negotiate the sale of a property, there are multiple offers in play, but they continually disclose competing offers to each of the interested parties. This is done in an attempt to force buyers to leapfrog the competing bids. The trouble is, of course, that you as the buyer at the end of the phone have no idea whether those other buyers actually exist or whether you're being played. The best way to avoid falling into the trap of getting caught up in making higher and higher bids is to know the value of the property you're offering on with confidence. Then you're less likely to get caught out by this practice.

HOW MANY PROPERTIES ARE FOR SALE?

In some locations, the most popular properties don't come up for sale very often and that means there is always strong demand from buyers for them when they do. What we're talking about are those houses or units in superior or desirable locations.

However, when market conditions are in the downturn or flat phase, more properties may come on the market more generally and in many areas, which keeps a lid on prices (the old supply-demand mantra!). By assessing sales and listing data, you can understand how many properties are currently available for sale.

One metric to help you is what's called days on market, which is the time it is taking for properties in a particular area to sell.

When the days on market are reducing consistently over a few months, this is a sign that there is generally more demand than supply, and when they are increasing, well, the opposite is true.

> **HOT TIP**
>
> Days on market stats can be a false friend. Remember that we also keep going on about different markets being exactly that ... different. Days on market figures will vary from one place to another. In some suburbs, taking 30 days to sell a property can be considered to be very quick, whereas in others it will leave everyone wondering why it's taking so long and what's wrong with it. Know the local market conditions in which you're buying to understand the difference.

As we have mentioned a few times, you should never try to 'time the market' because we believe you should buy when it is the best time for you, regardless of market conditions. That said, it is a good idea to understand this measure so it can help inform the price you are prepared to offer for a property, as well as how quickly you need to do so.

In rising markets, many properties will sell after the first open home or even before that, so if you spend a few days wondering what price you are prepared to pay, you may miss out entirely. Again, this is why we say you need to have done all of your necessary research and due diligence well before this stage so you can make an offer quickly if needed. It's like an iceberg — the pointy end is when you make an offer but there is a huge volume of research underneath your decision-making.

WHAT PRICE ARE YOU GOING TO OFFER?

By this stage, you should have all the necessary comparable sales and market research to help determine the price you are prepared to offer.

Having done all of this work, though, there is no point wasting everyone's time with a 'low-ball' offer, as it's called. If a property is listed for a certain price, and recent sales and market statistics support it, then there is little to be gained from submitting an offer that is well below this figure. The only thing that is likely to happen is the vendor will be insulted or the agent won't even submit it to them at all!

This can be the moment when your financial future is about to change for the better or it could be the moment when it might change for the worse. If you let your emotions overrule all of your due diligence and submit an offer that is far above market value, then you may reduce your future capital growth as well as negatively impact your ability to hold for the long term because of the higher mortgage repayments sucking your cash flow dry.

Working with qualified experts can assist you in this regard because they will have a much better understanding of the current market price for a property. Some buyers opt to engage a valuer to help determine the price of a property, but this is not necessarily a great idea as sometimes the assessed value is still below what the market would be prepared to pay for it.

At the end of the day, it is always better to miss out on a property than to overpay for it and spend the next few years (or even decades) regretting your decision. There is always another property that will suit you — and it could be next door or down the road from the one that you let go through to the keeper. We're not going to give you a formula to use for making an offer, because one doesn't exist. However, your offer price is really only one part of the equation.

ONLINE 'VALUES'

The computer-generated 'valuation' is another troublesome metric. Some websites and apps out there are designed to spit out the valuation of any property when you punch in the address. Please ladies, remember that a website isn't going to analyse the comparable sales in the same detail that a human will. It won't compare the state of the renovations of a property compared with next door, how nice the kitchen is, or the aspect and positioning of the block. Only a set of human eyes can do that. It also won't help you negotiate the right price for a property, because you won't know what you're talking about, and you won't know how to respond when the agent tells you that number such-and-such down the street sold for $50K more than you're offering. Don't be lazy. Do this due diligence and go into your negotiations with supreme confidence, armed with all the evidence, as only we ladies can.

DOES THE SELLER HAVE SPECIAL CONDITIONS?

Part of your due diligence must include understanding the seller's terms and conditions that are separate to their ideal sales price. What we mean is learning whether they are interested in a short or long settlement (the day the property ownership legally changes hands); perhaps they want to rent it back for a time, or would prefer to have a larger deposit from the buyer to show they are serious about purchasing the property.

Knowing what the seller's needs and wants are will help you craft the best offer possible because it might not be price that is the determining factor for the seller. Perhaps they are keen on a buyer who doesn't want to settle for a few months, so they have time to buy somewhere else themselves? Maybe they want to sell to an investor because they want to ensure their current tenants can remain in the property for the long term?

There are many variables when it comes to a seller's motivations, but you must do your best to learn what these are. The best way to do that is to simply ask the agent. They are usually more than happy to explain any special conditions the seller is interested in, which you can use to your advantage during the negotiation process.

HOW DO YOU PREPARE YOUR OFFER?

If we had a dollar for every time that we have heard someone say, 'But I offered X price when I spoke to the agent, but they sold it to someone else,' we'd have enough money to buy another property in cash!

While every major jurisdiction has different legal considerations when it comes to the purchase of real estate, verbal offers aren't really offers at all. They might work as a starting point when indicating to an agent that you are keen to purchase, but they don't generally fly when it comes to the formal mechanisms of legally purchasing a property.

Every female investor should have a decent understanding of how to buy property in their chosen location, because of the differing ways to do so from a legal standpoint. Your relevant state government (or similar) is an ideal place to start, as well as your real estate institute and QPIAs and conveyancers. You also need to understand what you can include in your offer, such as special conditions, or what actually may need to be drafted by a legal professional.

There are far too many variables when it comes to the legal buying and selling of property to list here, which is why we recommend you complete your own research or work with an expert team who can do this heavy lifting for you. Depending on the location of the property, the best way to submit an offer for a property is in writing, which can be via email, a form from the agent, or a contract of sale.

> **HOT TIP**
>
> **Buying property in Brisbane is different to buying property in Perth, which is different to buying property in Melbourne. Kate does this every day for a living, and can assure you that you don't need to be a legal expert to understand the different property-purchase processes in each state. Wherever you've decided to buy, know what the process is and what you can and can't do. And don't let these differences put you off buying in another state, either. This shouldn't affect any female investor's decision to diversify into another state or territory.**

Your written offer can usually be changed by mutual agreement by both the buyer and seller. For example, you might offer a certain price but the vendor counter-offers a different price, which you agree with and both parties countersign the contract. Finally, always keep in the mind the ideal buy-in price for you personally for all the reasons that we have listed so far.

If it's not the ideal price for the seller, don't keep upping the ante if you can't afford to do so. Rather, withdraw from the negotiation without burning bridges, because that agent may well be the agent on the next property you are keen to buy. In fact, sales agents can be very useful for buyers in particular locations because you are likely to have dealings with them a few times when you're actively trying to purchase in specific areas.

As well as never wanting to overpay for a property, you also don't want to get a bad reputation with the local agents who, let's face it, pretty much hold the keys to a property that can help create wealth, security and freedom through property for you personally.

Depending on the location where you are buying, different timeframes and differing processes will be needed for different things, such as cooling-off periods, finance approvals, and building and pest inspections. This is also true when buying at auction.

We could write a whole book about these differences (and we probably will), so our advice at this juncture is to thoroughly understand what the purchase processes are in that location, or work with an expert who knows this stuff like the back of their hand.

For example, don't come to any negotiations with a three-week need for finance approval in a Sydney market where a five-day finance clause before contract exchange is the norm. Likewise, in Brisbane, it is common for buyers to include a 14- or 21-day finance clause when signing a contract of sale — plus in Queensland, 'time is of the essence' rules the day legally when it comes to real estate transactions. This means that everything must be done by the certain date and time that is listed in the contract — although these can be renegotiated with the vendor by agreement and usually via your lawyer. So, in Queensland, the vendor can crash the contract if you don't get your finance organised in time.

That loan pre-approval that you secured (we hope) will enable you to buy within your budget with confidence, but remember it is not formal unconditional finance approval.

YOUR OFFER WAS ACCEPTED – NOW WHAT?

One of the most exciting times in a female investor's life is that moment when their offer has been accepted. All of that hard work has paid off and you have started making significant inroads into taking charge of your financial future. Woo hoo!!

After some well-deserved celebration, either with or without Champagne or beer, what happens next? Well, this is the time when all of your expert team members swing into action.

From that moment on, a large number of things need to be organised before settlement day, including your mortgage broker managing the finance approval for your loan application. You should also engage a local building and pest inspector to undertake this important part of the due diligence process. If there are major or minor issues with the property, you may have the opportunity to withdraw from the contract or renegotiate the price, depending on the situation and the property's legal jurisdiction.

At the same time, your conveyancer should start work on a number of legal checks on your behalf such as title searches, easements, covenants, local searches that include council rates and water rates, and many other legalities related to the sale and purchase of the land.

CASE STUDY: CHLOE'S STORY

Kate's lovely client Chloe has had quite the journey.

When she and her husband started out property investing, they were both in their early 50s. Some say that's a bit late to be starting out on your investing journey, but we say it's never too late as long as you start.

They had a plan, they'd been to a financial planner, organised their finance and were well on their way. And then her husband got sick. Things weren't looking great and they put the whole investing journey on hold while he was receiving treatment.

In spite of all the love and care and medical help, sadly, he passed away.

Chloe, grieving, had to get herself back on track and reconsider her priorities and plans.

Fast forward a year, and Chloe is now the proud owner of two investment properties. The day of her first property settlement, she cried out of sadness, joy and sheer relief. We think she's amazing for having come as far as she has and for not giving up on their dream of financial independence.

TO-DO LIST

- [ ] Get the full low-down on how properties are bought in your area of choice. Know what you're getting into.

- [ ] Be confident in your price assessment of the property. Check comparable sales so you can be an effective and successful negotiator.

- [ ] Ask questions and understand the market conditions as well as the seller's circumstances and needs.

- [ ] Develop your offer strategy. Make an offer that gets the deal done at the right price. They want to sell, and you want to buy. You both want the same thing. Sellers and agents are not the enemy.

- [ ] Get the deal done.

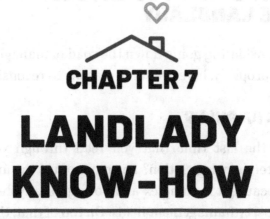

CHAPTER 7

LANDLADY KNOW-HOW

How to own property for yonks

This chapter is for our female investors who are embarking on their property investment journey as landladies.

As investors we love good property managers! They can make your life as an investor so much easier for all the reasons that we will outline for you. Alas, a bad property manager can add a huge amount of stress in your life, as well as cost you money, and we've both had that misfortune over the years. That said, just like any industry, there are far more good operators than bad, you just need to understand how to differentiate one from the other.

First, let's address an issue that regularly rears its head for novice investors, when they decide that they want to manage their property themselves, usually because they see it as saving money... oh dear!

6 REASONS WHY YOU SHOULDN'T BE A PRIVATE LANDLADY

If you are considering going down the road of managing your own investment property, here are some reasons to reconsider.

1. OODLES OF RULES

When was the last time that you read through your relevant residential tenancy legislation? For most of us, the answer would be never, because it is complex and boring for anyone outside the legal or property-management fields. On top of that, the legislation is prone to be amended regularly.

Renting a property to a tenant is a highly regulated environment to protect the rights of both parties. Plus, the rules can be different depending on which state the property is located in. If you fall foul of the laws, there can be significant financial ramifications.

2. TIME-CONSUMING

Many professional property-management agencies have top-level technology that helps them look after their rent rolls, as they're called in the industry. This means that they can stay on top of any repair requests as well as ensure that the legal timeframes are met when it comes to notice periods.

On the other hand, self-managing property investors generally don't have the systems, which means that they may well be the recipient of 3am phone calls because of issues that may be serious, or possibly not. If the issue is considered an emergency under the relevant legislation, do they even understand what they are legally required to do, and by when?

3. GEOGRAPHIC CONSIDERATIONS

As you've hopefully learned by now, we believe that female investors should buy in the best locations for them, which may not be nearby. If you purchase a property that is a fair distance by road or even by air from where you live, how do you intend to manage it from afar?

Attempting to self-manage a property that is intra- or interstate is set to be problematic because of the tyranny of distance. This also means that you are unlikely to have the necessary connections to local tradespeople who you can contact for assistance when needed and especially when a repair is urgently required.

> **HOT TIP**
>
> Property management agencies tend to have hundreds of properties on their rent rolls, and as such they have special arrangements and have negotiated good prices from tradespeople because of the sheer volume of work. If you're self-managing and you call 'Mick' the handyman (apologies for the stereotype, fellas) to do some odd jobs for you at your investment property, we can guarantee you'll be charged a premium for the one-off jobs. Way more than the money you're saving in management fees. It's truly a false economy.

4. WHEN TENANTS BECOME FRIENDS

One of the biggest problems when someone tries to self-manage their investment property is they become friends with their tenants when an arms-length relationship is always the best. New Zealand and Europe, for example, seem to favour a private landlord or landlady method more than Australia.

While it is always vital that you treat your tenants with respect, becoming friends with them when you are a private landlady can result in problems down the road. What we're talking about is when you decide to not increase the rent for a number of years and wear any additional costs personally because of your friendship. You may also find yourself approving things, such as alterations to the property, that would normally not be possible under the legislation, or recommended because it's an investment property and you shouldn't be overcapitalising.

You must always remember that your investment property is just that — an investment that can improve your financial future if you allow it to do so.

THE DANGERS OF NOT RAISING THE RENT

So, you don't want to charge market-value rent because the tenants are 'great payers'? Or you don't want to 'upset them' and are 'scared' of them leaving? While there are ways to reward good tenants, not achieving market rent can have serious consequences. Some of the negatives of not raising the rent in a reasonable way when you can do so include these: a lower cash buffer for those unexpected emergencies; the property may be viewed as less valuable by tenants and future buyers; once the rent starts falling behind the market in a big way, it is always difficult to do anything about it until that tenant vacates, which is why increasing the rents (to help cover your own rising property investment costs) is the smartest thing to do.

---

5. INCREASED VACANCY

By now we hope you understand that you should try to buy a property that will be in continual demand from tenants (and future buyers) for that area because it suits the demographics of the people who want to live there.

Property managers are local-area experts in their fields, which means they have a database of potential tenants for properties in their patch. Self-managing landladies, on the other hand, don't have the same reach, so they may have extended periods of vacancy after a tenant vacates their property.

Likewise, most tenants seek out properties on property-listing portals that are usually not available to private landladies or are very expensive. They may upload their property on second-tier sites that are often frequented by tenants who are unlikely to be approved under the normal checks and balances because of a poor rental history.

6. TENANT SELECTION

In a similar vein, do you understand how to screen tenant applications to assess who is the best fit for your property? The answer is probably not, right?

Professional property managers have vast experience when it comes to tenant selection, including checking references and rental histories, whether they can actually afford the rent, and whether the tenant has ever been blacklisted on special tenancy databases for serious issues in the past.

Most self-managing investors are unlikely to have access to the same information and may find themselves approving a troublesome tenant.

> **HOT TIP**
>
> Most property managers live and work in the area that your investment property is located in. They may have worked for other agencies, have family locally and they know people. Word gets around about troublesome tenants and they have local intel. They know things that you don't. Trust us.

We hope that you can see now why we always advise anyone, male or female, against trying to self-manage their investment properties — it is never a money-saver but rather a trouble-maker! The relatively low fees that property managers charge are worth every penny and can make the difference between owning an investment property for the short or long term.

WHY GOOD PROPERTY MANAGERS ARE ROCK STARS

Real estate agencies often have both sales and property-management departments; however, there are more and more property-management-specific real estate agencies around these days.

When it comes to agencies that feature both sales and property management, usually the best property managers work for the agencies that see their rent rolls as important to the overall success of their businesses. Alas, some sales agencies seem to only see property management as a cash cow that doesn't need to be nurtured or supported.

We've both had some rock-star property managers and some one-hit wonders in our property-investment journeys. The worst performers have been the ones who have been unprofessional and haven't looked after our properties to the degree that is even required by law. When it comes to the top property managers, well, you hope you can keep them forever because you trust that they are doing the right thing by you, your tenant and your property every day of the week.

So, what do good property managers do for investors? Well, it's almost a question of what don't they do?

PRE-PURCHASE INSPECTION

Before you purchase an investment property — especially in a different location to where you might live yourself — property managers may be valuable by attending inspections on your behalf.

Now, we're not saying that you can simply ring up a property manager out of the blue and expect they will do this for you! Working with experts such as buyer's agents and QPIAs will ensure this is not something you need to worry about personally.

However, if you are going it alone, then once you have selected a property-management agency (more on that soon), it's possible that they will inspect a property on your behalf before you buy as they will pick up the management of the property.

RENT APPRAISAL

Whether a property manager is assisting you before you buy or after — we recommend you make this connection beforehand — they will be able to provide you with a rent appraisal for the property.

As we've mentioned already, if the property is currently tenanted, never use this figure as the likely market rent, because it could be below it, or could be above it, depending on the market conditions and the supply-and-demand situation in that area. It's imperative that you understand the potential market rent as soon as possible so you can complete your cash-flow analysis. The property manager will also be able to negotiate a lease renewal with the current tenant once they have been officially appointed to act on your behalf if that is the best strategy for you.

If you purchase a property that is empty, the property manager can also assist with getting it ready for the first open-for-inspections. This can include managing minor repairs as well as updating appliances if needed.

HOT TIP

Like with the purchase process, tenancy laws are different in most states and territories. Certain amenities and facilities that a property has to have by law will be different in South Australia to Victoria, for example. Your property manager can help advise what minor upgrades the property may need to make it tenant-ready. Ideally you need to know this before you purchase so that you can factor these potential extra costs into your budget and cash-flow scenario. No rude shocks, please ladies.

SECURING A QUALITY TENANT

Fundamentally, a good property manager can secure you a quality tenancy for your investment. This will include promoting the property to their tenant database as well as promoting it on their own agency website and on other rental-listing sites.

Potential tenants generally have to register to attend the open-for-inspection, which also enables the property manager to easily keep them informed of any changes — such as a change to the time or date of the inspection — as well as keep a record of the people who have shown interest in your property.

Once applications have been received, they will then assess them to determine who are the best candidates for your property. Part of that assessment is that they have the financial means to pay the rent, but that is not the only determining factor. Property managers are also looking for tenants who have a stable history of renting, including looking after properties, which they evaluate via references.

Your property manager will then discuss the applicants with you, because the decision is yours as to who you approve as the tenants of your property. We generally accept the recommendation of the property manager because they are the professional and not us!

At this stage, you also need to consider whether you want to offer a six- or 12-month tenancy. Generally speaking, as long as you don't have plans to sell or renovate the property within the next six months, a longer lease agreement is usually the best option. This is because it gives you peace of mind that you will have regular rental payments coming your way, but it also reduces the fees associated with lease renewals.

Once the successful tenants have been notified the property manager will then prepare all of the necessary paperwork, which includes documents that have legal considerations such as the tenancy agreement. They will also ensure the tenant has paid a bond, which is usually equal to four weeks' rent, and is held by the relevant government residential tenancies authority.

DURING THE TENANCY

Once the tenancy starts, a good property manager will prove they are worth every cent of their fee. That's because they will manage all of the intricate details that are part and parcel of property management. Before the new tenants move in, the property manager will complete an entry condition report (and so will the tenants once they have moved in), which is a record of the condition of the property at the start of the tenancy.

After that, they will manage the ongoing aspects of any tenancy, including:

♦ Collect rent, disburse it to you and follow up any arrears, taking formal action if needed.

♦ Complete regular property inspections to check on the condition of the property and report back to you.

◆ Receive and action (with your approval as needed) any requests for repairs from tenants.

◆ Issue the required entry notices to tenants for any tradespeople who need to attend the property to complete repairs.

◆ Provide suggestions for the replacement of appliances as required.

◆ Issue regular rental statements so you have a record of the rent that has been paid.

◆ Facilitate entry to the property for other inspections allowed under the law, such as a valuer or a sales agent appraising the property.

◆ Manage the lease renewal process, including any changes to rent, as well as recommend whether to offer the current tenants an additional lease term of six or 12 months.

AT THE END OF THE TENANCY

Ask any long-term investor and we all say the same thing about the ideal tenants —people who treat the property like their home, who pay the rent on time, and who live there for a long time!

We've both had tenants like this — Nicola once had the same tenant who didn't really say 'boo' for eight years — but eventually they will move out and you will need to start the process all over again. Again, this is where your property manager will look after the entire process for you, including the completion of the exit condition report. If there are no major issues and the property is clean, they will organise the repayment of the bond to the tenant. However, if there is damage that is determined to be the tenant's responsibility, they can also organise repairs to be paid out of the bond.

Now that we have outlined many of the things that property managers do on your behalf, can you see why we believe they are worth every cent? You're probably wondering about how much they charge — and the answer is anywhere from about 4 per cent to 10 per cent of the weekly rent (generally speaking — a lot of variables may be at play, including geographic differences).

What that means in reality for any female investor with a property that earns $500 per week is about $20 to $50 per week, which is not only a very affordable price to pay for peace of mind, but is also tax deductible as a legitimate investment-property expense.

KATE TELLS:

BUSTING MYTHS

For those trying to save the above management fee by self-managing a property, just estimate how long it's going to take you to manage all those tasks that a property manager completes for you, traveling to the property and staying on top of everything.

Be honest, even if conservatively (but not realistically) you think you can get all that done in one hour per week, what is your time worth to you? I think we'll all agree that our time is worth way more than $25 per hour. And think of all the other things you could be doing, like researching your next property investment!

HOW TO FIND A GOOD PROPERTY MANAGER

It's vital that your property manager is a local area expert who understands the area's rental market inside and out.

So don't even consider handing your asset to a property manager who is miles away from where your property is located — even if they have been recommended to you. Not only will they not be an expert on the local rental-market conditions, but they are also literally too far away to be able to manage the property, including repairs, in a timely fashion.

A property manager should be part of your expert team, and the sourcing of the best one for your property is likely to come from recommendations from buyer's agents, QPIAs or local sales agents.

However, regardless of where the recommendation comes from, the selection of a property manager is another factor that requires research. If you're going it alone in an area that you aren't overly familiar with, you can start out by touching base with a few local property managers.

The ideal time frame is before you buy. Make a time to speak with them on the phone to discuss their potential appointment as the manager for the property you are interested in buying or that you have already purchased, and provide them with the address.

During the conversation, it is your opportunity to understand:

◆ their local and professional knowledge

◆ their property-management experience, including time at the agency

◆ their tenant-selection process

◆ how many properties they personally manage

◆ their communication methods, such as email, phone or text message, and which one suits you the best.

Essentially this is the time that both you and the property manager can determine whether you are a good fit for each other, which is imperative to give you the very best chance of owning your investment property for the years needed to achieve excellent capital growth.

Treat it almost like you would a job interview in that while a number of property managers will be able to fulfil this role for you, the best outcome is if you can have an open and honest relationship — especially when the going gets tough — more on that in chapter 8.

HOW TO BE A GOOD LANDLADY

The most successful property investors are the ones who do everything they can to hold onto their properties for a number of market cycles. One way they do this is by being a decent landlady.

Unfortunately, property investors wear more than their fair share of bad publicity and are often blamed for driving up the price of property when the savvy ones will never pay over the odds. As you know by now, emotional buyers — who are usually homeowners or owner-occupiers — are usually the ones who pump up prices. Alas, some property investors get bad press because they don't treat their tenants with respect or they don't address valid concerns such as necessary repairs and maintenance. It should sound like a no-brainer to anyone with, well, half a brain, but it is a legal requirement that a rental property is habitable and in safe condition.

One of the roles of your property manager is to always make certain that your property meets these minimal standards by ensuring that regular maintenance is completed, and necessary repairs are carried out whenever needed.

Ideally, you should aim to own an investment property that stands out from the crowd by being in superior condition and providing the bells and whistles that tenants and buyers in the area desire the most. These attributes can vary depending on the location, but consider things such as ceiling fans and air-conditioners in warmer climates as an example.

Again, your property manager will be able to provide advice on this for you before your first tenancy has started. It also imperative to understand that the condition of your property at the start of the lease must generally be maintained throughout. This means that you must keep up with necessary repairs and especially anything that is classed as an emergency, such as problems with electricity or water supply to the property.

By ensuring that your property is in tip-top shape, you are giving yourself the best chance of achieving a solid weekly rent for it, as well as attracting quality tenants who will want to stay.

We also believe that the best property investors are the ones who ensure the rent of their properties is in line with the market, but is also fair and reasonable for their tenants. This is especially the case for good long-term tenants, who should be rewarded for looking after your asset and making their rental payments on time week in and week out. But remember that this doesn't mean you should not raise the rent when appropriate. It's a fine balance that can be tricky to get right.

There is increased awareness now about tenants who have pets finding it difficult to secure rental properties. In years gone by, many investors simply didn't accept tenancy applications from people who had pets, but this blanket refusal is thankfully changing. We believe that, where appropriate for the type and size of the dwelling, you should consider allowing your tenants to have pets. Research shows that investors who do this are often rewarded with tenants who live in their properties for longer periods of time.

Some investors worry about the damage that pets can cause in a property. However, it's important to understand that tenants are responsible for paying for any repairs that are outside what could be deemed fair wear and tear. In Australia, you generally aren't able to charge an additional pet bond, but you will likely be financially compensated by the longevity of the lease.

When you embark on your property-investment journey, please do so with the best intentions, including treating your tenants with dignity and respect as well as ensuring your property is maintained to a high level. This will ensure that you are creating the ideal pathway to follow to hold your property for the years needed to help change your financial future.

By following the insights we have outlined so far, you will already be a strategic female property investor who has done everything she can to create wealth, security and freedom through property.

TO FURNISH OR NOT TO FURNISH – THAT IS THE QUESTION

One of the issues that investors often struggle with is whether to furnish their property or not. Now, this is usually reserved for people that have purchased high-rise apartments in capital cities, especially when there is the option of having the property in the short-term letting pool. The thing is, regardless of the property type, we believe that furnishing an investment property doesn't stack up financially. The financial outlay is far more than the better returns that you will supposedly receive. Plus, those furnishings will need to be updated sooner rather than later, which will be another expense likely to come out of your bank balance.

CASE STUDY: HALEY'S STORY

In spite of being in a long-term relationship, Haley is big into being proactive and taking responsibility for her own finances. She said she that was always surprised by the number of women she knows personally who are not involved in their own finances. They would say, 'Oh my husband pays for that' and 'My partner pays the bills'. They don't know how to set up a direct debit, and these are ladies in their 50s.

Haley wanted to take control. She was thinking of doing more for her future that would create an income stream. Something that wasn't risky and that she didn't have to monitor constantly that she could rely on as an asset into retirement, in addition to her super.

Now she's the proud owner of an investment property interstate, that she's never seen, with a great tenant and an excellent property manager who takes care of everything. Haley is so glad that she took the plunge. She feels that she has a sensible and low-risk investment, which will help create security later on in life no matter what happens.

TO-DO LIST

- ☐ Consider whether self-managing your property is really the best thing to do.

- ☐ Seek out an experienced (and awesome) property manager in your chosen area and use them to help you find your investment property, or use one of your expert team to do this for you.

- ☐ Remember that amazing tenants need fabulous landladies.

CHAPTER 8

HOW TO HOLD

Fear not, my friend

About 70 per cent of investors in Australia own just one property on top of their homes for myriad reasons.

Sometimes they don't feel comfortable with taking on any more debt, even though it is the good type that can help to improve their own financial futures.

Other times, it is because poor asset selection has reduced, or even eliminated, their chances of purchasing another property. This can be because they bought a dwelling type in a particular area that was oversupplied, and it didn't increase in value enough to extract equity to buy another property in any meaningful way.

Sometimes investors have overextended themselves financially by spending too much on a property and struggled to keep up with the mortgage repayments. Perhaps they have been side-swiped by a major repair that has eaten up all of their cash-flow buffer and left them broke. They may have also reached their lending ceiling with banks because their income, including rent, isn't high enough to sustain another mortgage in their name.

MAKING PEACE WITH INVESTING

Our wish for female investors is for you to take charge of your own finances and your own wealth creation by strategically purchasing property.

For many women, this may be just one property that they call home. For others, it may be purchasing a number of properties over a decade or more and then holding them for the long term.

Again, we want you to choose whichever strategy is the right one for you personally, but we also don't want you to be afraid of owning more than one property if you have the opportunity. Fear can starve you of opportunity and we believe that, when done correctly and with experts to help you, property investment is a low-risk option for many women.

One of the other reasons why so many people don't create a portfolio is because they get caught up in the regular fear-mongering in certain sections of the media. You know what we're talking about, don't you? It's those headlines that scream 'Property prices set to bust' or those current affair stories about 'The illegal meth factory at my rental property!' and the like.

Those stories no doubt achieve solid readership and audience numbers for their media owners, which is why they are trotted out all the time, but they generally do not have much basis in property-investment reality. Sure, there may be times when something extremely bad happens at an investor's property, but they are the exception rather than the rule in our experience.

Some other reasons why most investors own just one or two properties can be due to their misunderstanding of market cycles — not something that you will ever need to worry about because you have read chapter 3 of this book! That's not to say that when significant global economic events happen, like the GFC and COVID-19, it isn't a valid concern for investors, but having risk-management strategies in place should reduce your stress.

It's especially important during these times to remember that property is an asset class with a proven history of stable returns over the long term — including the rocky moments that we outline in greater detail later in this chapter.

THE PROPERTY SKY IS FALLING — ISN'T IT?

At the start of the GFC and the COVID-19 pandemic, the usual tropes were trotted out by so-called experts predicting that property prices were set to plummet by 30 or 40 per cent. During the GFC, one of the naysayers even said he would walk from Canberra to the top of Mount Kosciuszko — Australia's highest mainland mountain — if he was wrong. Well, two years after making the bet, he had to do just that.

Likewise, at the start of the pandemic, many economists, including the banks, were predicting massive property price falls. The opposite came true because of a number of factors, including record low interest rates. At the start of the first lockdown in 2020, PIPA was a contrary voice in the media when it released data showing that five years after each of the recessions or economic downturns in the past 50 years, capital-city house prices in Australia had often increased significantly and this situation was more likely than not to repeat again. No-one believed them at the time, but those investors who bought when others were fearful — during the first nine months of the pandemic — have achieved once-in-a-lifetime results over a short period of time.

Some property investors are prevented from growing their portfolios because they don't have the right loan structures that can assist them, while other times it is their well-meaning family and friends who become fearful for them and ultimately stop them from buying another property. There is no question that once you have finished reading this book and completed your own research via reputable sources and avenues — and especially if you have chosen to work with an expert team — then you will likely be much more educated than most of your friends and family about strategic property investment.

Never be afraid to forge your own path, because that is ultimately what we want, too — we want more female investors taking charge of their own financial futures so they can create their very own wealth, security and freedom through property.

Now, we need to change tack a little bit, because there will be issues that crop up during your property-investment journey that can seem scary at the time, but can be managed successfully with the right risk-management strategies.

WHAT TO DO WHEN THE SHIT HITS THE FAN

Let's be honest, you can't eliminate risk completely in any type of investment, and anyone who tries to tell you otherwise should be given a wide berth.

We're providing you with our honest opinions on the property investment sector so you can make informed decisions about whether the strategy is right for you or not. So we don't want to gloss over some of the downsides that can occur.

What can possibly go really wrong with property ownership? Well, quite a few things can happen and do occur from time to time, too. But we will provide you with a system to manage these risks, so please don't panic and throw this book at the wall or in the bin!

1. LONG PERIODS OF VACANCY

In a rental-market downturn, or in areas where there is far more supply than demand, your property could be vacant for several weeks or even months. One of Nicola's investment properties was vacant for 10 weeks once — ouch!

2. ONGOING MAINTENANCE AND REPAIRS

You should always keep up with regular maintenance and repairs, but sometimes a property might have a defect that needs fixing a number of times. This can be the case in smaller community title schemes, with the additional repairs sometimes needing to be funded by a special levy paid by each of the owners.

3. TENANTS NOT PAYING THE RENT

It's important to remember that tenants experience the same ups and downs in life, including job loss, as you do. Sometimes tenants may simply stop paying the rent — for legitimate or nefarious reasons — which is a situation that will need to be addressed as soon as possible, including taking the legal options to remove a non-paying tenant from your property (another reason why professional property managers are so valuable).

4. DODGY DEALINGS

Rarely, a rental property may be turned into a meth lab or dope-production den. Rental properties that have regular inspections are unlikely to be chosen for these illegal activities. The clean-up costs can be extraordinary.

5. GETTING SUED

Yes, that's right, there is the chance that you as the property owner may get sued by your tenants or their visitors for negligence or personal injury that may occur at your property. A horrific example of this was a balcony collapse allegedly caused by owners not undertaking the required maintenance or repairs to ensure their property was safe. Of course, this will not happen to you as you will be a good landlady and not a bad one!

6. DEATH OF A TENANT

Homeowners and tenants pass away in properties on a regular basis. Your property manager will be able to assist you with this as there are laws that must be followed if your tenant dies in your property. If the death is traumatic, like a murder or suicide, then there is the chance that your property could become stigmatised, which could impact its value to tenants or future buyers — although these events are extremely rare.

7. SIGNIFICANT PROPERTY DAMAGE

Your property might be in an area that has some sort of natural disaster risk, whether that be flood, bushfire, cyclone, or earthquake. Just like none of us wanders around worried about the risk of these every day, it is also a good idea to be informed about their potential impacts but not worry about them unnecessarily. Likewise, significant property damage can happen at rental properties, which may be the responsibility of the tenant or may be, for example, a fire from an electrical fault.

8. PEST PROBLEMS

Pests can be a problem at many properties, especially termites, rats, and even possums and snakes, depending on the location. Having a thorough building and pest inspection before you purchase the property is imperative, as is keeping up with regular pest trapping and treatment methods. Nicola once walked into her kitchen to find a possum sitting on the bench looking back at her — eek!

9. OVERPAYING FOR THE PROPERTY

All of these problems are things that can and do happen, but their risks can be managed relatively simply. However, if you overpay for a property to start off with, that is not something that can be remedied easily, except waiting for the passage of time to hopefully negate its impact on your wealth-creation efforts.

***

The problems we have outlined above are not regular occurrences, but it's better for you to understand them early than try to work out how to manage them later.

In reality, far less serious issues are likely to crop up at your property from time to time, which can be expertly handled by your property manager. These include:

- minor repairs such as a broken air con or a fence paling repair

- short-term vacancy of a week or two between tenancies

- tenants falling behind in rent for a week or two but then catching up

- a minor weather event such as a hailstorm, which results in some window repairs

- your tenant breaks their lease, but your property manager finds a new tenant quickly.

It's important to recognise that all of these issues would be handled by your property manager after discussing with you and gaining your approval as required, so that is why we always say property managers really are your 'sleep at night' factor. Another way to make sure you are giving yourself the best chance of holding your investment property or portfolio for as long as possible is to instigate risk-management strategies from the outset.

KATE TELLS:

MY VACANCY EXPERIENCES

Remember that property in a mining region I talked about in chapter 4? Well, that once sat vacant for nearly three months, because of local overdevelopment and an almost total drop-off in demand. The rent had already plummeted and soon all tenant enquiries dried up, too. The saving grace was that I had not overextended myself in terms of the loan and because cash flow on my other properties was good, it propped this one up until I did eventually get a tenant. I once had another property vacant for about three weeks, because of a much more minor blip in market demand, and I took this opportunity to paint, carpet and freshen up the place. This means I secured a good tenant without having to drop the rent because it looked nicer and cleaner than some of the other older properties on the market.

BEING READY – FOR ANYTHING

We want to educate you now on how you can minimise the fallout from all of these potential issues.

Firstly, it can take time for most investment properties to earn enough weekly rent to cover all of the related expenses — depending on a number of factors, including the purchase price. In fact, a PIPA investor sentiment survey found that investors generally believe it will take least five to 10 years before their property or portfolio could be classed as positively geared — that is, the income from the property covers all the expenses and has some left over.

So, how are you going to cover any potential cash-flow shortfall if that is your situation for a time? Now we're not going to give you a magic formula that shows you need to set aside 'x per cent' each week for your cash-flow buffer — this is an impossible calculation when we don't know your personal income or any potential shortfall between the rent and the property costs, including mortgage repayments.

However, any potential weekly negative cash flow should generally be managed and accounted for as part of your personal household finances and budgets. Bigger cash buffers should be there to cover big-ticket items (the shit hitting the fan); however, weekly cash-flow management will better enable you to hold on to the investment property over the long term.

Female investors need to complete this calculation prior to purchase, so you can assess the holding costs versus your ability to finance any shortfalls. There are many, many factors that affect how your cash-flow outcome will look, and this will vary from investor to investor, property to property, and area to area.

The cash-flow outcome will actually be different for the exact same property for two different investors. We recommend that you set up a good system and a spreadsheet that will do this calculation for you. You can also talk to your accountant or QPIA, who should be able to help you with this. You will also start to get the hang of it once you get going and do it a few times.

To start you off and give you some basic information, let's say that you're thinking of purchasing a freestanding property in your own name for $500 000, which will achieve $500 rent per week. Our example here has you paying cash for the purchasing costs (stamp duty, legal fees and so on) and a 20 per cent cash deposit on the property, so you'll be borrowing $400 000 at an interest rate of, say, 2.5 per cent on an interest-only loan.

The income is the easy bit: that's your weekly rental amount multiplied by 52 weeks in the year (or 50 if you want to be more conservative and factor in a two-week vacancy period). This will give you your projected annual income from that property. Allowing for the full 52 weeks, this will give you an annual rental income of $26 000.

To get your basic yield for this property you can then divide that income amount by the purchase price (some purists will want you to factor in all the borrowing costs too, but let's keep it simple for now).

$$\$500 \times 52 = \$26\,000$$

$$\$26\,000 \div \$500\,000 \times 100 = 5.2 \text{ per cent}$$

This calculation will give you a 5.2 per cent yield, and in property terms, that's not a bad yield. You can see that the less you pay for the property and the more rent you receive per week, the higher this basic yield will be.

This little ready reckoner won't give you your personal cash-flow outcome on your property, but if you know that 5.2 per cent is quite good, you'll know how to start assessing properties that you're considering purchasing.

To get a rough cash-flow outcome, you'll need to think about all the outgoings, too, which are your 'holding costs'. For our property purchase example this could look something like this:

- ♦ $10 000 annual loan repayments

- ♦ $3038 property management fees —at 8 per cent plus GST (goods and services tax) and lease fees

- ♦ $3000 council and water rates

- ♦ $1400 property and landlord insurances

- ♦ $1000 repairs and maintenance

You might also need to consider strata fees or land tax if you already own property in that state.

All these outgoings add up to $18 438. If you subtract this amount from your income of $26 000, that leaves you with an annual income of $7562. Now this is a positively geared property. This is taxable income but you're making money here, and that's not a bad thing, and not a bad return on your cash investment per year either. It's even better when you factor in the capital growth you are likely to achieve as well.

Let's change the above scenario a little to show you a different outcome.

Say we're buying a property, again for $500 000, but this time it's in a different location and it's now earning $350 per week in rent.

Do the easy income calculation first. Multiply $350 by 52 weeks in the year (or 50 if you want to be more conservative and factor in a two-week vacancy period).

Allowing for the full 52 weeks, this will give you an annual rental income of $18 200. And let's assume that you're still paying 2.5 per cent interest on your $400 000 loan, only this time you're making principal and interest payments.

This means that the annual repayment amount will go up quite a bit. To get your cash-flow outcome, consider your holding costs again. This time your figures would look something like this:

- ◆ $18 960 annual loan repayments (principal and interest — just use an online calculator to give you a rough guide here)

- ◆ $2127 property management fees (at 8 per cent, plus GST and lease fees)

- ◆ $3000 council and water rates

- ◆ $1400 property and landlord insurances

- ◆ $1000 repairs and maintenance

And don't forget that you might also need to factor in strata fees or land tax.

This time your outgoings add up to $26 487. If you subtract this amount from your income of $18 200, you'll get a minus figure of $8287. This means that the property is now costing you $8287 per year.

The difference isn't just that the rent is lower, and the property is costing you money — you're also paying down the principal loan amount with this scenario.

> **HOT TIP**
>
> We think that it can be really beneficial to work out the cash-flow outcome on any property using both an interest-only loan *and* a principal-and-interest loan scenario, regardless of what your actual loan type will be. That way you can see a true picture of how the property is performing as an investment without the principal payments getting in the way of your calculations.

Try this for yourself and vary the scenarios a little:

◆ maybe make a 10 per cent cash deposit and borrow more money

◆ vary the purchase price and rental-income amount

◆ allow for that two-week vacancy period with your income

◆ you might pay more or less in management fees

◆ you might pay less in repairs over the year.

The many different variations depend on the property and the area.

Other things will affect your cash-flow outcome, such as your personal marginal tax rate and the age of the property on which you may be able to claim a depreciation deduction. That's something to talk to your accountant and advisers about.

But, ladies, it's important that you go into each purchase with your eyes wide open, having at least a reasonable idea of what the property will cost or yield you.

HOLDING AND THEN HOLDING SOME MORE

When we talk about how to hold investment properties for the time needed to achieve significant capital growth, we mean at least 15 years. Yep, when you buy an investment property — or two or three or whatever suits you personally — really, we want you to hold on to those assets for as long as you can. And that is why having extra cash flow or financial buffers is so vital, because that can make the difference between being able to own these properties for a lengthy period of time or having to sell early. We explain more about why your portfolio must 'grow wrinkles' in chapter 11.

As we've mentioned previously, a property is an illiquid asset, which means you can't sell it quickly, for example if you run out of cash. It generally will take two to three months to sell a property, which likely feels like an eternity when someone has no capacity to pay the mortgage.

However, having a financial buffer can provide you with the safety net you need to ride out temporary downturns, such as extended periods of vacancy or unexpected job loss. The last thing you want to do is sell because you are in a financial black hole for a month or two. A financial buffer helped Nicola when one of her properties became vacant in the middle of a rental-market downturn — she used her cash-flow buffer to see herself through and would have lost $100 000 in capital growth if she had been forced to sell back then for the sake of $3000 lost rent. Of course, this was also the 'warty' property in her portfolio — you know, the one she bought when she really shouldn't have because it was not a strategic investment property at all.

Another risk-management strategy to keep in mind is the fact that interest rates will rise, and they will fall, during your investment journey. Please don't get fixated on these or worry about them unnecessarily, because the loan structure is more important. However, when the interest rates are operating in a normal lending environment, rising rates generally lead to higher rents, so it is nothing to fear. The propensity for rates to rise and fall is another reason why you should always charge market rent for your properties. Another option is to refinance your loan to another lender or switch your loan to a fixed-rate period for a time if you are concerned about your ability to pay higher mortgage repayments.

> **HOT TIP**
>
> An interest-rate rise will generally lead to there being fewer property buyers out there — investors in particular, as it makes property more expensive to hold. This in turn means that there are fewer properties available to rent, but demand remains high — because there's fewer buyers. You see the cycle of supply and demand? Less supply will lead to higher prices; in other words, a rise in rents.

PROPERTY MANAGERS – AGAIN

Yes, we want to talk about property managers again, because they are also a risk-management strategy for female investors.

Having an experienced and well-connected local property manager on your team can really make the difference between your ability to hold for the many years required — or not. Most of the potential problems that can pop up for property investors can, and will, be handled by your property manager.

◆ It is their job to secure you a great tenant as quickly as possible to reduce periods of vacancy.

- It is their job to remedy any rent arrears with your tenants and suggest solutions as needed.

- It is their job to manage repair requests from tenants, including organising the relevant tradespeople to complete the work.

- It is their job to conduct regular inspections of your property to ensure it is well-maintained and safe.

- It their job to recommend the market rent for your property for new leases or lease renewals, which helps hedge against future interest-rate rises and assists with accumulating your financial buffer to pay for unexpected costs.

WHY INSURANCE IS NON-NEGOTIABLE

We think that any property investor who doesn't have the necessary insurances is a bit of an idiot.

Clearly, a number of things can go 'bump in the night' for female investors over the decades, but most of these potential issues can be appropriately covered by insurance policies. An experienced insurance broker could be another person on your expert team.

There are insurance policies that can provide cover for unforeseen personal expenses, such as periods of illness, so you can ensure you can continue to afford to hold your property or portfolio if you can't work. Likewise, there are specific policies for property investors — unfortunately called landlord and not landlady insurance — which can provide funds to cover property expenses for specific circumstances as well as your more common building insurance. All of these insurances can assist with the 'sleep at night' factor during your property-investment journey.

BUILDING AND LANDLORD INSURANCE

For female investors who have purchased a freestanding house, you will need to have building insurance. There are many different policies out there, but please ensure that your house is not underinsured. That means that in the unlikely event that your property burns down, for example, you have enough insurance coverage for a new house to be constructed. A broker will be able to provide advice on this. If you buy a unit or townhouse, building insurance is paid for out of your body corporate or owners corporation fees so you don't generally need your own policy.

Every property investor should have landlord insurance — special policies that can provide protection for investors against tenant litigation via public liability provisions.

But it can also provide insurance cover for a number of different issues that can significantly impact your cash flow such as a tenant absconding from the property, malicious damage or theft at your property, as well as cover for your property's contents such as flooring. Again, there are many different policies out there, so it's best to do your own research and work with an expert insurance broker.

HOT TIP

Don't be afraid to call your insurance company each year when you get your renewal documents through and question and negotiate the hike in premium — and there will be a hike, trust us. While there may well be a genuine reason why premiums rise in a particular area, most insurance companies rely and thrive on the fact that almost everyone out there will simply renew automatically. It's how they keep making more and more money, even when you haven't claimed for anything. This is your precious cash flow we're talking about here so make the call, and tell them to offer a better rate or you'll go somewhere else.

Do you ever consider how odd it is that we usually insure our vehicles and our cars, but many of us don't insure ourselves? What we're talking about is income protection insurance that can provide funds to see you through when life takes an unexpected turn. In Australia, many of us have the ability to have some form of income protection within our superannuation, but it's vital to understand what this does and does not cover as well as any stand-down periods. That is, some policies won't provide funds for the first few months, which may be the exact time that you need them.

Likewise, other personal insurance policies to consider are life insurance and total permanent disability (TPD) coverage. Again, both of these are available within your superannuation or outside it in Australia. Both of these options can mean that you may have access to funds in the worst of times, when you need them the most to ensure your family, and your assets, are protected.

It is imperative that you recognise that our lives take many unexpected turns over the decades. While none of us know when or if our lives will hit a fork in the road, by having the appropriate insurance policies in place, we can have a safety net that we can draw upon in times of need.

It's a bit like the cost versus benefit of property management. Sure, insurance policies cost us money via premiums, which, don't forget, can be paid monthly, but they can make all the difference for female investors who want to be able to hold their investment property or portfolio for a number of decades.

We'd never want you to have to sell a property because you had a shortfall of funds for a temporary period of time.

While we outline the 'best' times to sell in chapter 11, the goal should always be to own your property for as long as possible and for as long as it is working for you personally. Anyone who is forced to sell one of their properties at a time not of their choosing is usually having to do it for negative reasons, which may cost them dearly in the years ahead.

KATE TELLS:

THE FLOODING

A property I have in Adelaide once had some minor flooding to the timber flooring in the lounge, because of a major rain storm that went through. The drains just couldn't cope – so water came into the house – and neither could the bamboo flooring, which was completely drenched and warped.

The tenants were great about the whole thing, and luckily my insurance cover paid for the entire $12 000 repair bill, apart from my $1000 excess. My insurer also paid for the tenants to be housed in a hotel for two weeks and even to move their piano into another part of the house!

The property manager handled the whole thing and all I had to do was give her my insurance details. While it was clearly not ideal, what could have been a major headache turned into not much of a drama at all. Plus, my tenants are still there three years later!

CASE STUDY: JULIE'S STORY

Julie's story is a typical one — the kind that just makes us want to weep.

Julie is in her mid-50s and when she came to Kate for advice, she was freshly divorced from her husband of almost 30 years. As the primary caregiver to their now-adult children, she had only had the odd part-time job here and there, and as a result had very little in her superannuation account.

As part of the divorce settlement, she got to keep the family home and was receiving spousal support for another couple of years. However, Julie was aware that she would need to work towards replacing this source of income. Relying on such a meagre amount in super and the state pension would not be an option if she wanted to still enjoy her life and not live in poverty in her twilight years.

Drawing down on equity from the family home and securing a loan with income from her part-time job allowed Julie to purchase a modest investment property. The property paid for itself from the start and would grow in value over time to help provide some much-needed security and top up her finances later in life.

Julie's grit and determination after an emotional relationship breakdown was nothing short of inspirational.

TO-DO LIST

- [ ] Make peace with all those pesky risks — most are rare occurrences.

- [ ] Get your risk-mitigation plan in place.

- [ ] Get yourself a red-hot local property manager onside.

- [ ] Think about and calculate what financial buffers you want in place for yourself.

- [ ] Make sure you know your weekly cash flow and have a management system in place so you're never caught off guard.

- [ ] Think about the various insurances and speak to a professional about which ones you need and want to put in place.

- [ ] Make sure that you can sleep at night. We can't overstate this.

- [ ] Never be afraid to forge your own path. You are on your way to true financial freedom!

CHAPTER 9

HOW TO IMPROVE

The reality of renovations

Some of the most popular shows on the telly for the past decade or two have been renovation ones. Millions of Aussies and Kiwis have sat glued to the TV as they watched seemingly novice couple after couple renovate rundown properties into real-estate superstars that they sold at auction for millions of bucks.

Plenty of investors have a dream to buy a 'fixer-upper', which they can turn over in a mere weekend or two then rent out for a much higher rent, and eventually sell for a record price for its suburb.

The only true thing about this scenario is that it is a dream. There is a big difference between completing a minor renovation on a property and undertaking a significant one that is likely to cost far more than you have budgeted.

Now, we don't want to poo-poo renovations—they can be a successful strategy to improve your property's value. What we do want is for you to understand what is involved in undertaking renovations on a property you own.

BUDGET BLOWOUTS

Whether you decide to renovate your home or an investment property, the first thing you must do is calculate the cost of the project. This includes all materials and appliances as well as any tradespeople you will need to complete the renovation.

The most successful renovations have been strictly budgeted, including having contingency funds for unexpected expenses, and have often been managed and completed by professionals. A mistake that some investors make is trying to 'save money' by doing everything themselves. Even though they never have picked up a paintbrush before or had any experience sanding timber floors, some investors seem to believe they will be better at it than experienced tradespeople who are paid to do it.

Of course, what often happens is the end result is so underwhelming that it reduces the potential rent rather than increases it. Sometimes they may even need to pay a tradie to redo it for them, which will put the kibosh on any savings they thought they were going to make by doing it themselves.

One of the major issues with self-managed and completed renovations can be budget blowouts because of unexpected expenses such as the cost of materials, labour hire and generally just spending too much on fixtures and fittings that are ultimately unnecessary. This is called overcapitalisation and is a real risk for novice renovators who spend far too much on a property for what it can ultimately return in rent or value uplift.

WHAT DO TENANTS WANT?

When considering a simple or cosmetic renovation for an investment property, it's vital to consider what tenants in your area want in their properties.

Most of the time, tenants don't care what brand of oven or cooktop is there — unless you have bought a blue-chip property in a high-end suburb. Rather, they want decent appliances that work. Likewise, in some locations tenants will want different things than they will in another part of the country. This is especially the situation when it comes to climate. For investors of properties in warmer climes such as Queensland, ceiling fans are non-negotiable, with air-conditioning units also usually a prerequisite for most tenants.

You must determine whether the property you are considering purchasing has the fixtures and fittings that tenants and future buyers want in that area before you buy it. If it doesn't, you must add these costs into your buying-expenses calculations so they can be installed before the property is rented out. This is another piece of market intel that local professional property managers can assist with.

IT DOESN'T MATTER WHAT YOU LIKE

When strategically investing in property (apart from buying your own home to live in) it doesn't really matter what you like — and especially when it comes to renovations.

Just because you have a favourite colour palette or a penchant for black-and-white tiles, it doesn't mean those aspects would be a savvy addition to your investment property. There is a reason why many investment properties have a similar look and feel, after all. That's not to mean that they look boring. But a crisp and clean interior as well as a well-maintained exterior, including gardens and lawns, will allow future tenants and buyers to imagine themselves living there, which is what we all want.

NICOLA TELLS:

MY LOVE FOR ORANGE

I love the colour orange, but you won't find anything that colour in any of the investment properties I own. My wardrobe? Well, that is a different story!

Here's the truth of the matter, though: I'm not a big fan of completing renovations myself at all. That's mainly because I am very bad at painting and many other pursuits such as hammering nails or sanding floors. Perhaps that's why I married a tradie!

I do have a red internal door in one of my investment properties that was installed when it was my home, but it also serves a purpose by stopping a draft from the interior stairs flowing upstairs into the living room. We're not saying no colour, but not too much.

---

4 SIMPLE COSMETIC RENOVATIONS

Say you've purchased an investment property, whether it be a house or a unit, but your property manager or your own due diligence tells you that it needs a little bit of love before you list it on the rental market. What simple cosmetic renovations can be undertaken at an affordable price?

Below we have listed four options, but there are many others. We don't pretend to be experts in the art of renovation, but there are plenty who can help you determine which updates or upgrades might be the best for you, your budget and ultimately your property.

1. INTERIOR PAINTING

Painting really has to be the one renovation that can completely transform a place from drab to fab. Old walls that are cracked and tired can be reborn using the skilful application of plaster and paint.

Now, it's not a mistake that we used the word 'skilful', because the opposite of a professionally painted interior is one festooned with paint drips and patches that make it look worse than it did to start off with! We always recommend working with qualified painters when updating the interior of your investment property.

The additional expense is actually a cost saving that will mean your property will not only look better, but will not need to be repainted for a good number of years. Your future tenants will be grateful that the interior really does look the best that it can if you have wisely chosen to use expert painters.

HOT TIP

Just like Nicola, who loves the colour orange but doesn't have it in her investment properties, you have to put yourself in a prospective tenant's shoes. If you've painted all the walls in the house mint green, or you've got a striking purple feature wall in each bedroom because you think it looks 'trendy', you're creating an immediate and massive obstacle to every single potential tenant and buyer who will be trying to imagine how their furniture and artwork is going to look in that home. Keep everything nice and neutral, so you don't turn off 95 per cent of tenants and it sits vacant for weeks on end or you struggle to sell the property when the time is right for you.

2. UPGRADING FLOORING

We don't know about you, but how many properties have you been inside, whether as a visitor or at an inspection, and the flooring is an abomination? Old threadbare carpets, tired vinyl or timber, or even mouldy tiles everywhere the eye can see — and all your eyes see is yuck!

Another cosmetic renovation that can be easily undertaken is to upgrade the flooring in your investment property. Many older houses in Australia and New Zealand have original timber flooring that has been hidden under carpet for decades. Likewise, the popularity of vinyl back in the 1970s means that there are still plenty of properties out there with 'delightful' vinyl flooring. Existing timber flooring in many properties can also be upgraded via polishing and reoiling or staining.

I'm sure you're not surprised that we recommend working with qualified flooring or renovation experts to undertake these upgrades because the risks of stuffing it up are even greater than they are when attempting to paint like a professional. In fact, if you make a big boo-boo trying to upgrade your flooring, it could be a very costly exercise indeed to have it fixed up by the person you should have paid to do it in the first place.

HOT TIP

Remember those pesky tenants and buyers again? Well, don't assume that everyone is going to want the same flooring that you think looks and is lovely. Many people love the feel of a lovely fluffy carpet under their toes when they roll out of bed in the mornings — yes, even in tropical Queensland. Kate has walked away from buying many properties for her clients because the bedrooms had tiled flooring. It's just not what most people want. Do your research and look at what the majority of other properties look like and then do that. Remember to keep it neutral and relatively low maintenance for your cash flow.

3. WINDOW FURNISHINGS

Now this cosmetic renovation is one of the easiest and most cost effective, but it's surprising how many investors don't do this.

Just think of where you live now — when was the last time you updated the window furnishings? For most of us, it's not done very often. However, it is a simple way to modernise a property and especially one that has mouldy curtains or blinds that no longer work.

As part of the wider update of the interior of your property, consider which window furnishings would add to its appeal, but which will also not create additional headaches for tenants. For example, most tenants prefer blinds of some description rather than curtains, which can become dusty and mouldy. Again, it's a good idea to consider using a professional to select and install these to ensure they fit the necessary spaces in the property properly.

4. LANDSCAPING

When we say landscaping, we don't mean getting Jamie Durie over to create some backyard brilliance, worthy of winning national gardening awards. No, we mean making sure that the back and front yards of your house look their best.

First impressions count, which means that potential tenants will likely have driven or walked by your property before they attend the first open-for-inspection. If the lawn is overgrown and the garden is in a state of disrepair, this will be a big turn-off for them — all they will be imagining is spending their weekends working in your garden.

Engage a local gardener or handyperson to sort this out for you before the photos are taken for your rental property's listing. Even better, retain this person for the regular upkeep of the lawn and yard, rather than expecting the tenant to do it.

NICOLA TELLS:

HOW I MADE $40 000 FROM A COUPLE OF TINS OF PAINT

I bought an Art Deco apartment in a groovy inner-city location a number of years ago. At the time, the bank valuation came in under the purchase price because of soft market conditions and the valuer missing the fact that it had a lock-up garage and exclusive-use courtyard. The low valuation was far from ideal and the valuer refused to change the val even when I pointed out the omissions – sigh...

I managed to renegotiate the purchase price down somewhat, but still had to tip in some extra cash to finalise the deal because I knew I would regret it if I didn't. Still, it pissed me off that the valuation was so low, so I did some research (thankfully I was editor of *Australian Property Investor* at the time) and, over the course of a few weekends, painted the existing, super-ugly brown kitchen cabinetry white and installed a few sturdy shelves. Like I said, I'm not a painter at all, but at the time I needed to do the best I could.

My efforts (which weren't as bad as I thought they would be) not only modernised the kitchen instantly, but also made it appear much larger. Not long after, I paid for another valuation, which came in $40 000 higher than the previous one as well as being well above the purchase price I had only just recently paid.

MORE SERIOUS RENOS

The above cosmetic renovations will help you to maximise your rent potential as well as uplift the overall value of almost any property. But we need to talk about the elephant in the room — or maybe it's two elephants in two rooms! What we're talking about are kitchens and bathrooms.

Even the best 'spit and polish' of the interior will not hide the fact that the kitchen has an orange-tiled splashback (yay, says Nicola!) that was sexy in the 1970s but is not (alas) any more. It probably still has a freestanding oven with stove elements that many a young hand had been burned on back in the day — and lit parents' cigarettes when needed, too.

In the bathroom, there is every chance it could be pink, mint green or even purple — complete with multicoloured tiles on the walls and floor. It might also have an unused bath taking up most of the floor space and not an extraction fan in sight.

Now, depending on what type of person and female investor you are, you will have either smiled with delight on seeing the opportunity or screwed up your nose and promptly walked out the door. Nicola used to be the latter, mainly because she has no interest in renovating personally, but thankfully her husband does it for a living.

There is no question that kitchens and bathrooms are two of the most important spaces in any property for tenants and buyers. No one wants to spend time in a kitchen with appliances that are mostly obsolete or even faulty, or in a bathroom that's dark and dingy with tiny shower recesses with weird frosted glass that attracts mould.

Upgrading kitchens and bathrooms doesn't come cheap, but is always a sound idea for a female investor keen to maximise a property's tenant appeal as well as its future sale price. Again, it's vital that you work with experts to guide you on what would be best for your property as well as for your budget.

For those investors who purchase a timber or rendered house, there is also the possibility that its exterior will need a paint job, or its render will need to be replaced and repainted. Sometimes it just has to be done if the paint is peeling off and will be a turn-off for most people, as well as cause unnecessary damage to the exterior.

These types of works can also be costly — especially if the original paint is lead — but are worth every penny in our opinion. Not only will it make the house look fresh, but the paint will also protect the timber from rotting. Ideally, you should aim to paint the exterior of a timber home every decade. This type of work should be completed prior to tenants shifting in, either before your first lease or between leases, to reduce the impact on their lives.

KATE TELLS:

IS IT WORTH DOING?

You may have heard the term 'feasibility study', meaning working out whether a project (large or small) is financially viable or not.

When it comes to any type of renovation (or development, for that matter) you need to assess whether the money you're about to spend is worth it. There's little point in spending $10000 on a great renovation that will only increase the weekly rent by $20 without really affecting its value. But it can definitely be worth spending a couple of thousand dollars increasing the rentability of a property by making it more desirable.

Think before you spend and get your spreadsheets out, ladies.

SMALL PROPERTY DEVELOPMENT

An advanced strategy to improve a property and its value is via small property development. Although this book is a beginner's guide for female investors, we thought it was necessary to discuss small property development briefly — many investors try these strategies far too soon and usually end up financially worse off because of it.

When we say small property development, we mean anything that will structurally change your property or the block of land on which it is (or was) located.

If you follow some of the big names in the property-investment sector, you will often hear them talk about opportunities to subdivide blocks and build a secondary dwelling at the rear, construct duplexes on the site, or even knock down an existing home and develop four or five townhouses on the lot.

All of these options are potential money-makers — for people who know what they are doing and who have tonnes of experience behind them! That's why we say it's an advanced strategy.

There are so many hoops to jump through from a building and development approval process, plus the sheer cost of undertaking most of these projects, that most investors, whether male or female, would be wise to give these a wide berth until they have plenty of experience.

> **HOT TIP**
>
> Remember our best friend the town planner from chapter 5? Well, they are about to become almost family. They will be able to tell you what you can and can't do to a block of land. It's always worth having that conversation with them when you're conducting your research because they will point you to the plethora of council planning policy documents that you'll need to read through, understand and be familiar with before you can do anything — or get one of your expert team to do this for you.

To help create that experience — for those who have a higher risk profile and who have time on their sides as well as cash flow — it can be a good idea to project-manage a few cosmetic renovations, and perhaps then move on to a few alterations or additions to one of your existing properties. Don't forget, your expert team will be your most valuable resource in these matters.

Perhaps it is then time to target properties with land that can be split in two now (or in the future, as long as you have done your research), then you could either sell the subdivided and titled vacant land at the rear or next door if split down the middle (which costs money) or you could construct a secondary dwelling on it (which costs much more money) and rent it out or sell it.

These sorts of developments can produce excellent profits, but they are also considered high risk, which is why we don't recommend them to anyone unless they have plenty of property-investment experience and are working with experts to help maximise the potential from the project, but also minimise the risks.

CASE STUDY: ROSIE'S STORY

Rosie is the mum of a young teenager with autism. She has also had a number of health issues herself, all of which she has now thankfully overcome. Her son's father is no longer on the scene.

All of her life experiences gave her a real motivation, and a kick up the backside, to sort out her finances and get a financial plan in place, so the two of them wouldn't have to worry later on in life.

Rosie owned her own home, so she had some good equity to draw on. She was totally focused and single-minded in her approach and spent the next few years amassing a portfolio of 13 – count them ladies – 13 properties!

It hasn't all been plain sailing with that number of properties, of course, but Rosie has weathered every storm, never losing sight of the ultimate goal – wealth, security, and financial freedom. There is also a new man in her life now, and having done all the hard work, they can relax a little while her portfolio's growth works its magic.

Now, we don't all have to own 13 properties, of course, but Rosie's grit and determination to provide for herself and her son's future is a mindset that we can all learn from. Rosie, we think you're amazing.

TO-DO LIST

- [ ] Dig deep and consider whether renovation or property development really is something you're ready to do.

- [ ] If you've decided 'yes', then seek out trusted and reliable professionals to help you.

- [ ] Don't assume you know what's best in terms of style and features. Do your research to determine what will make your property more desirable and ultimately more valuable.

- [ ] Do a feasibility study on every single project you're thinking of starting, so you go into it with eyes wide open.

CHAPTER 10

HOW TO GROW

Having 'the talk'

You will now have a property-investment strategy that will suit you personally because of your age, your income, your marital status, and your wealth-creation goals.

If you are restarting on the property-ownership path after relationship breakdown or the death of a partner, we hope that the insights you have learned will help you to purchase the very best property to call home for you and your children and their children, too.

If you're under 30, we hope we have inspired you to take charge of your financial future sooner rather than later so that you are providing your own safety net in the years to come. This is partly because statistics show you're likely to have chosen, or will choose to be, the primary caregiver of your children, which may put you on the back foot financially for the rest of your life.

Of course, if you're in a relationship that lasts the distance, this splitting of familial duties will make no difference in your retirement years together as you are likely to be equal owners of any property or portfolio that you have grown together.

Unfortunately, though, a significant percentage of marriages still end in divorce, with an even higher percentage of second marriages not lasting the distance either.

According to the Australian Bureau of Statistics, the median age of divorce has been increasing over the years, with the median age for women in 2020 nearly 43, compared to 38 back in 2000, and for men it was about 46, up from about 41 in 2000.

Some of the reasons for this are likely to be people marrying later in life as well as having children when they are older, too. But the time frame of the 'average' divorce does seem to coincide with the moment when both women and men are nearing the peak of their earning capacities — as long as they haven't had years out of the workforce looking after children, mind you. The median length of marriage at divorce was also found to be about 15 years in 2020.

So, we can take away from these statistics that many of us may find ourselves divorced after a decade or two of marriage. Hopefully, during that time you have bought a home with your partner, and hopefully that property has increased in value over that period. Of course, given that market cycles don't happen with a regularity that anyone can predict, some people are experiencing relationship breakdown with a property that may not be worth as much as it was when they bought it. Or it may have only risen in value by a negligible amount because its location was inferior to start off with.

You can see why we spent so long on the intricacies of when, where and what to buy now, can't you? Even if you are using this information to help you select the best property for you and your partner to purchase together, that is a win — you will be both be better off financially because of it. If you're a younger female investor, we hope that you embark on your own journey when you are single, which will ensure that you have more choices and options later on in life.

Now, we are not here to argue who deserves what financially when relationships break down. But we want you to have created your own wealth through property — before you marry for the first, second or even third time! There is no judgement from us on how many times you want to say 'I do'.

But, say you have purchased a property or two before you met the love of your life, what happens next? Here are some strategies to consider.

PROTECTING YOUR ASSETS

We are not legal or accounting professionals, but we do have them on our expert teams for when it comes to conveyancing, and also for personal advice when needed. We believe that both parties in a relationship should protect any assets they have accumulated before they partner up so that each person has equal financial footing at the start of the relationship.

Prenups (prenuptial agreements) are commonly called Binding Financial Agreements (BFA) in Australia. They set out the financial terms of a relationship — preferably before you are considered domestic partners or are married, but they can happen after as well. The thing with BFAs, though, is that they can be very expensive, so you will need to work out the cost–benefit analysis.

At the very least, we recommend obtaining independent legal advice on your options if you have, or your partner has, accumulated property prior to the relationship, regardless of whether you decide to proceed with a BFA or not. It's also a good idea to ensure that you always pay for your investment-property expenses with your own income, and possibly via a different bank, to secure your independent ownership of them throughout the relationship.

> **HOT TIP**
>
> If you are a woman who is bringing more wealth to a relationship than the other party and they refuse to sign an agreement – or they are not happy with you wanting to protect the assets that you have worked so hard to accumulate before you met them – are they really the right person for you at all? And vice versa.

THE POWER OF TWO

Those of us who have grown a portfolio as a single woman know how many sacrifices we have had to make along the way, as well as the limitations that we may have had to work with during our journeys.

At some point, though, after you have met your significant other, there will come a time when you need to decide whether you will join financial forces or not. You can choose from several ways to do this:

◆ you buy a property together using joint savings

◆ either of you uses equity (more on that later in this chapter) for the deposit

◆ one of you sells a property that you bought before the relationship to help finance the deal.

This is a decision that you will need to make in collaboration with your partner. However, if you feel like you alone are being forced to finance your joint property, then it is probably not a good idea.

NICOLA TELLS:

JOINING FORCES

I bought three properties when I was single, but never quite had the income to purchase a house in any of the locations that I had determined were strategic investment locations. Even though I always bought the best units or townhouses that I could in those locations, it annoyed me that I didn't have a house on land in my portfolio. At the time, I was trying to purchase as close to the city as possible and a single income just didn't cut the mustard in those areas.

A few years after I got married, I chose to sell one of my properties to finance a property with my husband, who had previously been a single father. That was my choice alone and one that I was happy to make.

Not long after, we also bought a house together on a monster block of land — clearly, I was making up for not having a house in my portfolio before! Plus, I still own two investment properties separate to my husband — and he has no qualms about that at all... and nor should he!

Regardless of which way you decide to go when it's time to join forces, securing your own personal financial future could mean that instead of selling your investment property, you extract equity from it if needed. That way the property will still be yours and yours alone — and will be available for you should you need it at some point in the future.

We hope that we can help create a new generation of female investors who have financial independence from their partners when they need it the most.

Never again do we want a woman to be stuck living in a house with a partner even though the relationship has broken down beyond repair, or is stuck in a domestic violence situation, because she can't afford to move out or she literally has nowhere for her and her children to go.

Never again do we want a single woman in retirement living in poverty because her personal income never recovered from the years she spent raising children, just before her marriage ended in divorce.

And never again do we want there to be such a financial power imbalance in relationships — with one party always seeming to do better than the other at the end of the road — because they can afford better lawyers and never had time out of the workforce.

If female investors have their own property or portfolio that they either retain independently, or leverage from, during a relationship, then we will finally be heading towards a financial equilibrium point that most of us have never really had before.

OWNERSHIP STRUCTURES

A very important member of your expert team is your legal representative, because they can provide advice to you on the ownership structure options available.

This is a vital consideration for any female investor considering joining forces with your partner and purchasing property together. There are a number of different ways that you can own property, including joint owners, tenants in common, and via trusts.

Owning property in trusts is a complex strategy, so we recommend you speak to an accountant who is an expert in property investment — and preferably a QPIA — about that option.

> **HOT TIP**
>
> Some investors are lured into purchasing properties through a trust because they think it can 'offer excellent tax benefits and asset protection'. We're not saying that this isn't so, but it isn't so for everyone. You must have a clear understanding of what role a family trust plays in property investing, and you need to speak to a trusted professional who can highlight the pros and the cons. Don't go with someone who simply 'sells' you this idea of asset protection because they make money out of setting up the ownership structure for you.

JOINT TENANTS

The most common ownership structure is joint tenants, which is when both parties are equal owners. It's a legal term, not to be confused with actual tenants who are renting the property you both own. Both people will be on the title as half-and-half owners of the property, which generally means that any sale profits should be split down the middle if you were to separate. There is also a right of survivorship. This means that if one of the joint tenants (owners) dies, the property will automatically pass to the surviving joint tenant (owner). This isn't always the case, but we're talking in general concepts here.

TENANTS IN COMMON

The other option is a structure called tenants in common (in Australia at least). This is where each party owns a specified percentage of the property by agreement. Couples who opt for this structure are often doing so because one person is tipping in more deposit (or all of it) than the other.

For example, say you are purchasing a property for $700 000 with your partner. They may not have any funds to put towards the deposit but will have no problem paying their share of the mortgage. In this instance, perhaps a fair system is that the person who is paying for the deposit owns a greater share of the property legally.

Therefore, using a tenants-in-common structure may mean that one person, possibly you, legally owns 65 per cent of the property, and the other party owns 35 per cent. If you want to continue with this split, you could also pay this percentage of the mortgage repayments as well — although both parties are equally responsible when it comes to making sure the mortgage is repaid.

This type of structure can be a way to ensure that your additional input is recognised from a legal standpoint, but may create some future issues as the years go by and you are both paying for property upgrades and the like. Also, a tenant in common can sell their 'shares' in the property or give them away in a will. This means that there is no right of survivorship, which is the main difference compared to owners in a joint tenancy.

However, one of the benefits of this structure is that your proportion of the property remains yours. You can do it with what you wish, such as sell to your partner at some point and exit the relationship; receive this percentage of the property's value after sale; or even gift your share to another party after death (such as to your estate or your children from another relationship).

As you can see, though, this is an ownership structure that requires legal advice, so please make sure you speak with your legal rep before deciding whether this is the right way for you or not. On the day that you join forces with your new partner, hopefully you will start the next phase of your life on equal financial footing — and that's a win-win for women and men alike!

> **HOT TIP**
>
> ## Preparation is the mother of success
>
> We just want to stress the importance of having all your ducks in a row before you run out there into the sunset and buy property together. When you're in the euphoric phase of having your offer on a property accepted and the conveyancer sends you a form and needs you to confirm what ownership structure you're buying in, you may be tempted to gaze at each other lovingly and write 'joint tenants' while holding hands. All well and good and long may it last, and not to sound too negative, but what if that turns out not to be right for you? It's a hugely expensive fix, so make sure you're well informed and have all this thought through and talked through beforehand, so you avoid awkward conversations at the eleventh hour.

HOW TO EXTRACT EQUITY

Do you sometimes wonder how anyone owns more than one or two properties when it was such a struggle to save the deposit for your first one? Well, it's because of the power of compounding growth and the ability to extract equity to invest in property.

We've been regularly highlighting to you the importance of buying a property (or growing a portfolio) that has the very best chance of increasing in value. That rise in value — capital growth — in turn creates equity that can be recycled into another property.

For this to happen, though, you generally need to have purchased the type of property in a strategic location that is primed for growth over the short to medium term. Remember market cycles in chapter 3? You can never rely on a rising market cycle to do the heavy lifting for you. Rather, you can futureproof your chances of value uplift by making sure you buy the right property in the right place to start off with.

Over the passage of time, your property has likely increased in value to a certain degree. Say you purchased it for $500 000 using a $450 000 loan. In five years' time its compounding capital growth rate of 7 per cent per annum may see its market value at about $700 000.

Now before you go yippee, I've got nearly $250 000 I can use to buy something else, we are sorry to say that the banks don't let you completely denude your property of its equity! Sorry to be the bearer of bad news! The only way to extract most of that equity is to sell it, but we don't recommend you do that for some time (as we will cover in chapter 11).

The reality of the situation is that your investment property probably now has an LVR (loan-to-value ratio) of 65/35 — meaning the mortgage reflects about 65 per cent of the assessed value of the property — if you have been making interest-only repayments on the mortgage. Of course, this is an amazing result given you may have started out with a 90/10 LVR just a few years before!

Like all things finance, different lenders allow you to do different things, including how much of your equity they will allow you to extract out of a property to buy another one. Some lenders will let you borrow right back up to that 90/10 LVR mark all over again, but we don't necessarily believe that is the right option because it is not keeping 'enough skin in the game' for risk-management purposes.

Rather, we would recommend that a female investor in this situation considers using the equity that is available by taking the loan back up to an LVR of 80/20.

In this scenario, then, the available equity is about $110 000 — that is, the difference between the original loan of $450 000 and the new loan after equity of $560 000 is extracted.

$$\$700\,000 \times 80\% = \$560\,000$$

$$\$560\,000 - \$450\,000 = \$110\,000$$

Remember how difficult it was to save that first deposit, which probably wasn't anywhere near this figure? Well, here you potentially have a 20 per cent deposit on a $500 000 property being funded out of your first strategically selected investment property. Of course, you will still need funds to pay for costs, such as stamp duty and legal fees, but most of the funds will be available via this equity extraction.

Once again, there are numerous ways that this can be done and we recommend that you sit down with your expert mortgage broker long before you decide whether you want to use equity to start growing, or adding to, your portfolio. Another common way to do this is to top up the existing mortgage on the property to extract the funds for the next property. Another option is to refinance to a different lender entirely for the higher loan amount, especially if this may bring additional benefits such as better loan features and a more competitive interest rate.

Actually, speaking of refinancing, for those female investors keen to grow a multiple-property portfolio, we would recommend 'spreading the love' among different lenders. We suggest this so that you can retain better control of your property investment plans and goals. If one bank has all of your loans, then there may come a time when they simply say 'no more' and you will have to go through the hassle of refinancing some of your portfolio to another lender.

One thing to keep in mind is that everyone eventually has a lending limit of sorts, even when the rent from an additional investment property is added to your serviceability calculator, and even when you have loans with multiple lenders. The banks all know who you're borrowing money from and some will care about that, and some will care less.

A downside to spreading yourself across multiple lenders is that you're less likely to be able access better discounts on your mortgage rates. The more money you owe them, the better customer you are, and the better the interest rate on offer. So, there are pros and cons to all of this.

The moral of this story is, again, sit down with your mortgage broker and discuss what's best for you now and for the longer term. We've said it before, mortgage planning is much more important than simply the next loan you're looking to secure. Be strategic, ladies.

Sure, the goal should always be to buy the best you can, each time strategically extracting equity to purchase another property — either by yourself or with your partner — and then, when the time is right, do it all again. But the banking systems in Australia and New Zealand are so robust for a reason, including the many checks and balances that every buyer must endure every time they purchase a property, which is a very good thing. This means that our banking system is unlikely to ever suffer the same fate as what happened in the US before the GFC — when they were lending money to people who simply could never afford to repay the property loans in the first place.

While this section of this chapter has been predominantly about growing a portfolio, we don't want you to think that we are recommending you need half a dozen to make a big difference to your financial future. No, by purchasing the best property you can — and keeping in mind our advice on when, where and what to buy — you have already made significant inroads into creating wealth, security and freedom through property.

If you can do that a few times, well, even better!

CASE STUDY: MOHANA'S STORY

Mohana first came to Kate for some property investing advice some time ago.

She's a single professional lady, now in her mid-40s, with big plans to retire early and travel the world. They hatched a plan to purchase some properties over time, where the cash flow was manageable and wouldn't affect her lifestyle too much. Of course, she also wanted to go for good capital growth. So, her properties as well as her growing super account will give her some real options further down the track.

Five investment properties later, this awesome female investor is well on her way to not just true financial independence, but real wealth and freedom.

TO-DO LIST

- [ ] The love of your life has arrived, but you do need to have 'the talk'.

- [ ] Protecting your property assets is important — decide how you're going to do this and get some good legal advice.

- [ ] Moving forward and growing your portfolio needs to be planned and thought about. Decide how you're going to do this together.

- [ ] Think about how you're going to keep on financing property purchases, together or alone, and discuss this strategy with your finance professional well in advance.

CHAPTER 11

WHEN TO SELL

Why your property must grow wrinkles

Imagine this. A young female investor decides to buy a property when she's in her 20s and is earning a modest income, but it's enough. She purchases a two-bedroom unit that suits her budget — either in her home town or elsewhere. She might live in it for a while or rent it out straight away.

A few years later, she meets someone special and they decide to live together. Her new partner also owns a property, but they decide to create a new home in a neutral place, so they are on equal financial footing from the get-go.

Not long after, they buy a property together by each using equal funds, drawn from their respective properties, for the deposit. They agree (perhaps via a legal mechanism) that each person owns an equal share of that property, regardless of what happens in the future.

Perhaps they have children, or maybe they don't, but after a decade or so, the relationship has reached its natural conclusion. The break-up is messy, like these things often are, but one argument they hopefully don't need to have will be about 'who gets what' when it comes to proceeds from their jointly owned property.

They have that agreement they made when they purchased that property together, plus the female investor also has her original property that she has retained ownership of, and kept financially separate from her partner, throughout their relationship.

Depending on her circumstances — and after receiving professional advice — she may be able to buy a new home with the sale proceeds of the jointly held property; she might move into that original property (once the lease has expired); she might sell it; or she might extract equity from it again to purchase a new home for her and, potentially, her children. She might even buy her partner out of the home that they bought together. But her decision will depend on what is the best thing for her to do personally and financially at that point.

However, what she will have are financial choices. As time goes on, and she retains that one investment property over the years, her financial situation in retirement will be far better that it would have been without it.

Of course, this is the ideal situation because life is rarely so linear and clear-cut. It's just as likely that her new partner has no funds to put towards the deposit on their new home and they will need to decide what is a fair division of ownership.

There is no right or wrong answer to any of this, by the way. Nicola jointly owns properties with her husband who had no funds for the deposit, but he puts in plenty of 'sweat equity' as a tradie and she owns property separately as well. Whatever is the best outcome for you and your partner is the right path for you both.

The key here is the retention of that first property, preferably separate to the new relationship, for as long as possible to ensure you can create your own wealth, security and freedom through property.

A lot of people think it's a good idea to hold on to a property that they've lived in, and turn it into an investment property, and then buy a new property to live in.

While it can certainly be something to consider, depending on your circumstances and loan structure, this isn't always the best strategy. Remember that investment debt is currently tax deductible in Australia — because you're incurring the expenses from an income-producing asset — whereas your owner-occupier debt is not, because it's your home and therefore not income-producing. You may have paid this owner-occupier debt down over the years.

So what happens when you keep that home and turn it into an investment property and then buy a new home to live in, is that you now have a large, non-tax-deductible debt on the new home and a smaller, now tax-deductible debt on the old home that's become the investment property. We call this your loans being 'upside down'.

Also, you need to consider the fact that the home you used to live in might not actually be in a great investment location.

You may be better off selling that old home and buying your new home with the proceeds, while also keeping your non-tax-deductible debt as low as possible. Then you could draw down the equity and buy a new, true investment property. We know that life doesn't always work out perfectly, so talk to your tax accountant and mortgage broker about what's best for you. There are ways to structure your loans whereby both options are still possible.

But don't keep your old home for sentimental reasons. You need to be brutal with your decision-making — it always has to make investment sense.

LONG-TERM STRATEGY

Property investment is not a 'get rich quick' scheme, because that is just speculation masquerading as something else. Sure, there are times in market cycles where homeowners and investors can achieve above-average capital growth in a short period of time — 2021, for example — but these sharp uplifts are the exception rather than the rule and not something that anyone can truly predict.

Generally speaking, market cycles never run for a particular length of time, nor is the oft-repeated 'property prices double every seven years' true for every dwelling or for every location. Some properties in some areas may in fact triple in price in seven years, but others may do nothing at all. To improve your chances of buying a property that has the potential for sustainable capital growth, the very best you can do is to learn where and what to buy each time — and maybe repeat the process a few times if you are financially able to do so. By buying strategically, you will have a property that will be in strong demand from tenants, but also will be attractive to future buyers when it comes time to sell.

Speaking of selling, the subtitle of this chapter refers to the fact that you should try to own your property or portfolio for as long as possible (hence the wrinkles reference) — but without it significantly impinging on your finances or on your life. You should try to do this because time in the market, as well as asset selection, is likely to make the biggest difference to your future financial position.

Historical property data shows property prices generally increase anywhere from 5 per cent to 7 per cent on average each year — but it's important to understand this is when we look at the trajectory of prices over a number of decades.

Let's consider some excellent research from CoreLogic in the *25 years of housing trends* report by mortgage broker Aussie.

According to the data, in the 25 years to 2018, the Australian national median house value increased by a whopping 412 per cent! Back in 1993, the typical house value was about $111 500 and grew by an average of about 6.8 per cent to be $571,400 by 2018 — an average dollar-value increase of almost $18 400 per annum.

Now, can you see why we are hoping that our younger readers can hold on to their properties for as long as possible? Even for female investors who are restarting their property journeys, owning a property or two for a decade or two can make a significant difference to your wealth-creation efforts at retirement.

The report also states that some areas performed better than others over the 25 years to 2018, with Melbourne actually experiencing seven separate periods where house values increased by more than 10 per cent per annum. Its annual growth rate over that specific quarter century was 8.1 per cent.

At the other end of the spectrum, Brisbane and Adelaide produced the lowest annual capital gains, at 5.9 per cent, with the report saying that the diversity in growth rates over a long period of time highlights the cyclical nature of the housing market, with dwelling values rising at different speeds from region to region and from period to period.

'For example, despite Brisbane recording one of the lowest rates of annual capital gains, the period between 2001 and 2004 saw Brisbane house values rising at more than 10 per cent per annum; the lower rate of long-term growth is largely attributable to softer conditions since 2010,' the report said.

So, over that 25-year timeframe, most markets had periods of conditions where prices were soft, flat or rising, but when the ups and downs are ironed out, the end result was the significant increase in value of housing for all locations.

UPS AND DOWNS AND SIDEWAYS

While reading all these facts and figures here, it's important to note that the capital growth you get from property does not happen evenly every year. You won't get exactly 5 per cent or 7 per cent, or whatever it is, exactly every year. It'll be higher one year, lower the next, nothing at all the year after that, then maybe higher again and so on. This is why holding property is a long-term investment. You need to be able to ride out all the ups, downs and flatlines of the market and give it time to perform.

What this tells us is that to be a successful female investor, you must keep your eyes fixed firmly on the horizon and never get caught up in what markets are doing. Who cares if the market where one of your properties is located is a bit flat for a time? It makes no difference to you, your tenant or your property because it's just a moment in time — unless you are forced to sell. Plus, if you have purchased the ideal property in a strategic location, market conditions are likely to resemble Teflon rather than the *Titanic* when it comes to the impact on your property or portfolio.

At the start of the GFC and the COVID-19 pandemic, too, fear drove many people to sell their properties and we're sure they all regret their decision-making now. That's not to say that these periods weren't stressful — especially when it was initially implied that investors needed to provide free housing for their tenants during lockdowns, which was not a situation that came to pass. What we're trying to say is that you must have the fortitude and bravery in some ways to look past any short-term upheavals, because you understand and believe that property investment is a long-term wealth-creation strategy.

WHEN IS IT TIME TO SELL?

We're not big fans of the property-investment concept of 'Hold and never sell'. Ideally, we'd like to change this to be 'Hold for as long as it works for you' instead!

In every female investor's journey, the optimal moment will come for you personally to sell. This is an individual decision for each of us. Ideally, we would like you to hold on to your properties for as long as possible, but how long that will be is up to you and the unique circumstances of your life.

We haven't talked much about property taxes in this book because they are not consistent in every country. However, there is one that we must discuss for our female investors in Australia and that is capital gains tax (CGT). No one likes paying CGT, but it does mean you have made a profit on your property!

This is where your accountant will be able to provide you with expert advice, but generally speaking an investor will need to pay CGT on the profit from the sale of their income-producing property. According to the Australian Taxation Office (ATO), CGT is the tax you pay on profits from selling assets, such as an investment property.

To put it simply, a capital gain is the difference between the amount you paid for your property (less any fees incurred during the purchase) and the amount that you sold it for (less any fees incurred during the sale).

Although it is referred to as 'capital gains tax' it is part of your income tax. It is not a separate tax. You report capital gains and capital losses in your income tax return in the financial year that you have sold the asset and you pay tax on that capital gain.

If you sell your property in less than 12 months from when you purchased it, you'll pay the full capital gain at your marginal tax rate. But, you (as an individual) could get a 50% discount on your capital gain (after applying capital losses) for any CGT asset held for over 12 months before you sell it.

So that means that here in Australia, as long as you have owned the investment property for more than 12 months, you may be entitled to a 50 per cent discount. A large number of other variables can impact the CGT you may have to pay, which your accountant can explain to you in more detail. The ATO does have plenty of information about it on its website too — ato.gov.au.

When becoming a female investor, it is vital that you have an accountant who is an expert in property investment on your team and that you speak with them before you start your journey.

Most of the time, none of us can predict when we might choose, or need, to sell a property but if you can time it for a period when your personal income tax is low — such as after retirement — this may reduce the CGT you will have to pay.

Here are some moments when you might decide to sell an investment property.

1. UPGRADING YOUR HOME

For those of us female investors who have been around for a while, the property we live in now is the not the first one we bought. Rather, over the years, we have been able to trade up to better properties because we purchased that very first one that has grown in value over the years.

As we mentioned in chapter 2, Nicola sold her first property to pay for a deposit on her dream property and also extracted equity out of her third one to pay for an investment property with future subdivision potential — all in the same year!

However, one time when it might suit you to sell a property is when you want to leverage the proceeds into a superior one to call your home and you may not want to retain the investment for whatever reason. Again, there is no right and wrong way to do this because it is a personal decision for you to make.

At the end of the day, life is for living, so there is no point living in a substandard property with a large portfolio, when you could sell one and buy a better one or even purchase your dream home!

2. REDUCING DEBT

As we mentioned in chapter 2, at some point the mortgages on your property or portfolio will need to be repaid. For female investors, your weekly rent payments will do most, and hopefully all, of the heavy lifting over the life of the 25- or 30-year loan. But, having said that, a property that's earning you an extra $30 or $50 per week is nice, but it's not going to pay down a $500 000 loan any time soon; you'll need to have a more significant loan repayment strategy to really turbocharge paying down your investment debt. A healthy, positive cash flow on your property will simply cover your repayments and holding costs and enable you to own it for the long term.

However, sometimes it might be necessary to sell a property to pay off another one at some point. This is the strategy for many successful investors who purchase a number of properties, say six, hold them for as long as possible, and then sell down three over a few years (although you do not want all those CGT events in one year!) to hopefully pay off the mortgages of the remaining three. By doing this, they have created significant income from the properties as well as retaining ownership of them, too.

We're not suggesting this is a strategy for you because only about 15 000 people in Australia actually own six investment properties or more — our very own Kate is one of them! But it's a sound strategy to consider for those female investors who have the ability to perhaps own two or four rental properties over their working lives — Nicola has four … and more to come, too!

3. CREATING CASH FLOW

You may be one of the female investors who, in fact, never sell their investment property or portfolio in their lifetimes because they wish to gift it to their children or their estate, which is a perfectly reasonable thing to do.

Others may decide, at some point — perhaps when they are semi-retired or retired — that the time is right for them to sell their investment property or portfolio. Let us be clear, we are not suggesting selling the home you live in, as that will make all of the difference to your retirement. However, by selling your investment property or portfolio and reinvesting that money somewhere, you will be creating cash flow, in addition to your superannuation funds, that can make you a self-funded retiree — an outcome that we dream will become a reality for more women as soon as possible.

As it stands now, there are restrictions (in Australia at least) when it comes to who qualifies for a pension in retirement, with successful property investors unlikely to meet the criteria — and that is a good thing.

A significant percentage of single women in retirement live in poverty, surviving week to week on the pension, because they probably have to pay rent out of these meagre provisions as well. Data in the Australian Government's *Women's economic security in retirement insight* paper shows that the number of elderly women experiencing homelessness increased by over 30% between 2011 and 2016.

- More elderly women than men are living in poverty in Australia; contributing factors include the gender pay gap and superannuation savings gap.

- Being single increases the risk of poverty.

- It is more common for women than men to live alone.

We want to help put an end to that happening in the future.

We want women — of all ages — to go on the front foot with their retirement planning by using property as a vehicle, so they never have to worry about how they are going to afford food or medications or have enough money to visit family in their twilight years.

It is shameful and it needs to stop.

We hope that by reading this book and by taking action that you will help us make that happen. Together, we can change our own financial futures. Let's do it!

SOME FINAL WORDS FROM NICOLA AND KATE

Phew (mops sweaty brow and tired keyboard fingers) — that was quite the journey, wasn't it? We've tried to cram as much in as possible to set you up for your property-investing journey.

You may need to go back and revisit sections and chapters here and there and go through your to-do lists, but whatever you do, you need to make a start. You need to get out there and do this, because if we can promise you anything, it's the fact that there will always be a million reasons (in a Lady Gaga kind of way) you can think of not to do this.

What we mean is it'll be too hard, too expensive, life will get in the way, there'll be world events that put you off like GFCs, pandemics, hurricanes, floods and who knows what else this world has in store for each one of us.

Now, very few of us actually want to make, or have, a gazillion dollars. We sure can all think of a lot of things we'd do with that much money, but most of us just want to know that we've provided for ourselves, that we're not going to be living on beans on toast every night, or too scared and too poor to put the heater on when winter arrives each year. We just don't want to have to worry about financing our lives and our retirements.

We just want enough money during our lives to be financially secure and independent, pay the bills, go on a trip or three every year, support the kids if we so wish as they grow up, go to uni, and start families of their own, don't we?

So, imagine if Sally met Harry or Harriet once she'd bought a couple of investment properties. Imagine being able to sleep easier knowing that you have an investment property or two sending rent money into your account every month to repay a mortgage on a capital-growth asset that is also increasing in value over the years.

It can be tricky to talk to other people about all this. Many of us aren't used to talking about money. It can be a taboo subject and if you are brave enough to bring it up, you may be bombarded with a thousand different opinions, warnings and no doubt some horror stories, too.

It can also be quite confronting when you know someone who is seemingly way ahead in their financial planning than you — someone who's apparently really got their shit together. Someone who owns their own home, has a great job, has a great lifestyle, and has properties and investments falling out of their ears. That can be intimidating and can make you retreat even more into procrastinating about making a start yourself at all.

But here's the inside info on that one — if they're super vocal about it, sometimes things are amiss. Sometimes it's all bluster and bravado, and she is just a scared and anxious little pixie like the rest of us. Things are not always as they appear.

So, don't lose heart. Most importantly, don't make those soul-destroying comparisons. You don't know what's going on over there. Remember that everyone's story is different. Everyone has a different financial situation as well as differing hopes and dreams.

Whether you're in a relationship but your other half isn't interested in purchasing property or you want to forge out on your own (yay!), you know you need to get your investing butt into gear, stat. Likewise, whether you're single and loving it, whether you're married, divorced, widowed or a single parent — you know you need to take charge of your financial future.

So, here's our rallying cry: to be a successful female investor you need to be strong, motivated and completely clear on why you're putting yourself through this journey. Because it is hard work. There's no sugar-coating here. It's easier to run out of steam, hit roadblocks and give up than it is to stay motivated for the long haul — which is what's required. You need to keep at it, but we know you can do it.

You need to always keep an eye on the prize so by the end of it, you'll have made massive inroads into securing financial independence, amassing real wealth and the Holy Grail — creating passive income as well as freedom from working for a living.

Getting qualified advice from your peers — from likeminded women who have similar goals — is so important. You must have the support and encouragement you need to go ahead with your plans, to keep you motivated and forging ahead. We are here to give it and we are honoured and proud to be part of your journey.

We know the whole idea can be overwhelming, so we've given you lots of handy hints and steps to take. We want to get you started and motivated for the short term, so that you're set up for life regardless of where that takes you. And if you've already started, then high five to you lady, you're awesome and keep going!

Reread this book because no matter how many investment and finance books you read, it takes a lot to stay motivated and on the right path these days. There's a truckload of white noise and scary media stories out there. There's no such thing as reading too many books that educate and inform you about this subject, as long as that's not all you do — you do need to take action as well.

So go and reread our book, head to thefemaleinvestor.com.au and our podcast, go and buy more books, listen to some great podcasts, and talk to your girlfriends about what they are doing to provide for themselves. There are so many fantastic women out there who are helping other women, who are qualified, ethical and honest, and who have a real interest in helping you. Women who will help you be smart and independent with your money.

We are so very grateful that we got to spend this time with you. We hope to have inspired, motivated, helped and encouraged you into taking action. We promise that getting on top of your finances can be one of the most rewarding thing you'll achieve. You'll be so darned proud of yourself and we will be of you, too. It's also all about getting off your butt, stepping up to the plate, and getting this stuff done.

Take action now! Go forth and invest wisely, ladies, so you can change your financial future and create wealth, security and freedom through property.

And never forget, we're right there with you ... every step of the way.

INDEX